I0031959

Fit to
Practice

Everything you
wanted to know about
starting your own
psychology practice in
Australia but were
afraid to ask

Kaye **Frankcom**
Bruce **Stevens**
Philip **Watts**

AUSTRALIANACADEMIC**PRESS**

First published 2016 by:
Australian Academic Press Group Pty. Ltd.
18 Victor Russell Drive
Samford Valley QLD 4520, Australia
www.australianacademicpress.com.au

National Library of Australia Cataloguing-in-Publication entry:

Creator:	Frankcom, Kaye, first author.
Title:	Fit to practice : everything you wanted to know about starting your own psychology practice in Australia but were afraid to ask / Kaye Frankcom ; Bruce Stevens ; Philip Watts.
ISBN:	9781922117779 (paperback)
	9781922117786 (ebook)
Subjects:	Psychology--Practice--Australia.
	Psychology--Practice--Australia--Handbooks, manuals, etc.
	Psychology--Australia--Methodology.
	Psychologists--Australia.
Other Creators/Contributors:	
	Stevens, Bruce A., 1950- author.
	Watts, Philip, author.
Dewey Number:	155.2

Publisher: Stephen May
Copy editing: Rhonda McPherson
Cover design: Luke Harris, Working Type Studio
Typesetting: Maria Biaggini, The Letter Tree and Australian Academic Press
Printing: Lightning Source

Contents

Chapter 5

Where do you belong? Consultation, supervision and professional support and self- care   53

Chapter 6

Ethical dilemmas: traps in private practice land   63

Chapter 7

Tricky and complex presentations in private practice   71

Chapter 8

Feedback Informed Treatment (FIT): how to and why you should implement it in private practice   85

Chapter 9

Record keeping, case notes and writing reports   99

Chapter 10

Chapter 11

Chapter 12

Psychology comes of age

Psychology as a profession has come of age. A psychologist is now part of a professional group that has a status within the health professions and the community at large. The discipline of psychology attracts a lot of interest in Australian universities, with undergraduate units proving very popular and the demand for entry to, for example, Clinical Psychology Masters programs greatly exceeding available places.

The landscape of contemporary psychological practice changed dramatically in November 2006 and again in July 2010. These two dates delineate changes in the status of psychology as a profession with shifts in the role of government and regulations affecting the practice of psychology.

The Australian Government began to address the disease burden of mental (ill) health. It funded the Better Outcomes in Mental Health Care program through GP Divisions to provide psychology services through private psychologists. The program then morphed into the Better Access to Psychiatrists, Psychologists and General Practitioners through the MBS (Better Access initiative) that introduced new mental health Medicare items on 1 November 2006 thus enabling people with diagnosed mental disorders to access services from a range of mental health service providers, including psychologists. So for the first time in the history of the psychology profession there was an opportunity for Medicare subsidised services.

Private practice, which traditionally was seen as the territory of psychologists with many years of experience, suddenly became a financially viable option for many if not most psychologists. This level of government support has made private practice a possibility for any registered psychologist.

This book is a manual for those who are starting out in private practice or have questions about how to operate in that context; for example:

- How do I find a way of working in private practice that utilises all of my skills and training but is time efficient and financially sustainable?

- Private practice seems ideal: You work for yourself, and when you want to, and develop your own approach and speciality. What is the down side to private practice?

- Setting up a private practice from a business perspective is not something I was taught in my training. How do I do this in a way that it is financially effective for me without compromising my clinical practice?

- I have experience with high prevalence disorders such as depression and anxiety but I am not sure what to do with clients who have personality difficulties or substance abuse or health problems. I am not as confident to work with chronic pain, eating problems or cancer. When should I refer these cases to others, but still develop my practice and satisfy referrers?

- I am not sure when to go into private practice — all of my peers are doing private practice work and appear to be overwhelmed at times, while others don't have enough referrals. I have been registered for two years, have a Masters of Counselling Psychology and have worked mainly in community health settings. When is the optimum time in your career to go into private practice?

This book will provide some answers to these and other common questions for anyone setting up a private practice in Australia. The authors all have years of private practice experience as well as other experiences: academic training, dealing with complaints about psychologists, training and supervision of provisional and registered psychologists, as expert witnesses, and leaders in the profession.

There are now a number of organisations that offer training in private practice development, but there is no text to back up the professional development process required to be a successful psychologist in private practice.

Hopefully, this book will fill that gap.

Ms Kaye Frankcom
Professor Bruce Stevens
Dr Philip Watts

Chapter 1

The basics: Life since Medicare

History and context

We, as psychologists in Australia, find ourselves in a changing context of professional practice — largely not one of our making. So it is important to fully understand recent shifts if we are to survive and flourish as a profession.

In Australia, as of December 2014, there were 31,982 fully registered and provisionally registered psychologists of which 78.82% were female and 21.18% were male (Psychology Board of Australia, 2014). It is predicted that one third of our group will have retired or have reached retirement age in the next 10 years. The biggest specialist group, by endorsement, are clinical psychologists who numbered 6,873 (Psychology Board of Australia, 2014) but they tend to be unevenly spread across Australia with most in Victoria and New South Wales. The great majority of clinical psychologists continue to work in the larger population centres. We know this because we now have a national register for psychologists (and indeed for all the other registered health professions).

Until 2010 neither the government nor the community had an overview of the psychology workforce. We did not know how many psychologists were practicing in Australia, where they worked, what sort of work was done or their geographical location or principal place of practice. The picture was 'muddied' by multiple jurisdictions, legislation and registration standards.

Prior to this The Council of Australian Governments (COAG) sponsored the Australian Health Practitioner Regulation Agency commonly referred to as AHPRA, National Registration and Accreditation Scheme (*Health Practitioner Regulation National Law [Vic] Act 2009*), which became the operational body of the Psychology Board of Australia, referred to as PsyBA. Prior to this the Australian Psychological Society (APS) was our only national body and was expected to represent the profession to the various government bodies. The APS now boasts over 22,000 members and like all professional associations has a political agenda aimed toward promoting the interests of its members. In establishing the PsyBA, government(s) signalled a power shift. The PsyBA is now the body that registers and endorses psychologists, and determines such things as eligibility for clinical psychologist status. PsyBA has a contract with the independent accreditation body, the Australian Psychology Accreditation Council (APAC), for accrediting courses leading to registration to practice as a psychologist. The APS, our professional association, continues to be a key source of information and is the lobbyist for the profession but they are no longer the gatekeepers.

Since July 2010, there have been some key changes for psychologists in Australia. There are registration standards to which all psychologists must adhere. These standards include continuing professional indemnity insurance, expectations about professional development (passive/active and peer review/supervision), and expectations of English language competencies (see www.psychologyboard.gov.au). These changes came about because psychology, like the other 14 registered health professions, is considered to be a profession whose practices could be harmful to a person and thus require greater regulatory standards.

The APS achieved a huge milestone in 2006 when the Federal Government announced that psychologists would have Medicare item numbers. This was the result of many years lobbying on behalf of the profession and the community. It has been a bittersweet outcome. The Department of Health and Medicare established a two-tiered system: clinical psychologists with scheduled fees, and reimbursement rates 25% higher than their colleagues (which included all other psychologists regardless of qualification, specialist training, or APS college membership, etc.).

Reflect: What changes have you noticed in recent years? Can you think of concrete ways these changes have impacted upon the way in which you practice?

Key Learning Points

- There are a number of pathways to registration as a psychologist. The 4+2 pathway (four years academic, two years professional training in the workplace) continues to co-exist with Masters and Doctorate programs as methods of obtaining registration. There is now a 5+1 option that has a year of professional training leading to generalist registration.

- Clinical psychologists are the best renumerated psychologists under Medicare.

- If you are thinking of upgrading your qualifications, or are finishing your undergraduate or honours year and wish to work in private practice, health, counselling and clinical psychology Masters and Doctorates may be the most universally useful qualifications to achieve. Admission is highly competitive with importance placed on undergraduate and honours grades.

- Psychology is a diverse profession currently without a developed and government-recognised specialist base of medicine (in comparison with a specialist such as a cardiologist who practices only in his or her speciality). This may change in the future but the diversity of psychology is currently under pressure with the closure of some tertiary courses such as community psychology, sports psychology and health psychology.

- Psychology is unique in the health professions as it is both a discipline or knowledge base and an area of practice. Many students undertake 1 to 3 years of psychology at university, being exposed to the discipline, but never go on to practice. Psychology can be a knowledge base for other professions within the sciences and humanities fields. Marketing; for example, draws on psychological principles of motivation and change.

- The APS and the PsyBA perform different functions in our profession and practice. You must be registered with the PsyBA to call yourself a psychologist and to enter practice. It is a 'protected title'. Terms reflecting specialist endorsement such as 'clinical psychologist' are also protected titles and are not to be used unless you have an endorsement in this area of practice with the PsyBA. The APS is our Australian Medical Association (AMA) — it is a professional association that supports and promotes psychologists, a lobby group and also a watchdog for many issues that are relevant to the psychology profession. These issues include mental health policy, legislation and accreditation of courses. By belonging to your professional association (whether it be the APS or one of the alternatives), you keep in touch with what is happening in your profession and are connected to the standards and mores of that profession, the latest research and thinking in many fields related to psychology and have access to a variety of resources such as databases and continuing professional development (CPD).

Keeping out of trouble

Some of these changes have been welcomed by psychologists. Fletcher et al. (2011) looked at the attitude of private psychologists to the Better Access to Psychiatrists, Psychologists and General Practitioners (Better Access), an Australian Government initiative, and found that in general psychologists reported positive experiences. Psychologists have appreciated the greater security of income and variety of work afforded by the initiative, and they have observed flow-on benefits in terms of increased access to, and reduced stigma towards their clients. What the authors did not mention was that along with the increased numbers and demand for services, there is an increased risk of complaint. There is also a risk of lowered standards of service when psychologists are under pressure to respond to referrals. Many recent entrants into private practice have a limited understanding of the business and clinical models an accompanying standards required to support them in their endeavours to work effectively with their clients.

The APS Code of Ethics has been foundational to the practice of psychology in Australia. Training in ethics begins at university and continues in practice. This code has been recognised by the PsyBA. But what does it mean in private practice situations?

One way of understanding the risks is to examine instances of breaches of ethics or codes of conduct. These often become known of via complaints to the boards.

There have now been a sufficient number of complaints against psychologists over the last 20 years or so that we have been a registered profession to recognise some general trends in (un)ethical practice. In terms of practice, we know we should avoid dual relationships with clients, however complaints about boundary violations have been estimated at little more than 9%. Instead it is the issue of poor communication that is cited in 35% of complaints (Grenyer & Lewis, 2012). In fact the top three categories of complaint were:

- poor communication standards
- professional incompetence
- poor business practices.

This was found in an Australian study of 4 years of complaints to the New South Wales Psychology Board. The authors also drew the conclusion that, over a 30-year career, 20% of psychologists should expect to be the subject of a complaint by a client.

Reflect: Think about how you would feel if a complaint was made? Who would you talk to? How would you manage the process?

The 'good news' is that we can make clinical decisions to maximise our effectiveness and avoid trouble in the form of complaints. This includes the client reporting to their GP that you are not making a difference, or complaints to a regulatory body that will investigate any conduct, performance or competency issues raised by the complainant. Clients will often present for treatment saying something like:

> *The previous psychologist was nice and listened but nothing changed, I wasn't helped as to what to do next. It was good to talk about my problems but that was all that I got out of it.*

What is often missing is a rigorous assessment process that includes standardised tests, a treatment plan, and a feedback-informed approach to psychological treatment that enhances the therapeutic alliance and creates commitment to the change process and achieving the goals that have brought the client to therapy.

Key Learning Point

- Although the Medicare Better Outcomes in Mental Health Care program has created access to psychology services for all, it has not necessarily meant that clients are any more motivated to change or enthusiastic about the work involved in addressing the psychological difficulties in their lives. Clients can attend in a pre-contemplative/contemplative state (Prochaska, Norcross, & Krebs, 2011) where they are ambivalent, avoidant and even ignorant of their difficulties but have shared their problems with a GP who has then written out a Mental Health Treatment plan and told them that they are eligible for 'free' psychological treatment. When this type of client walks into a private practice, there is a great deal of work to do to assist them to re-think their current behaviour and move towards a position of reflecting on the need for change (and who or what needs to change). All of that will need to be achieved in 10 or fewer Better Outcomes funded sessions!

The shaping of practice in Australia

As a result of these social forces, private psychological practice in Australia operates on a brief (in session number terms) therapy model. In addition, this brief therapy model requires a 'mental disorder that is diagnosed by a GP'. The APS website notes 'The mental health Medicare items for psychologists' in Table 1.1 on the next page.

Note the exclusions as a primary diagnosis of personality disorders and relationship problems. The registered psychologist must utilise 'focused psychological strategies' or risk Medicare audit sanctions. These psychological strategies are listed on the Medicare Benefits Schedule — Allied Health Services (Department of Health, 2012, p. 50) as follows:

1. psycho-education
2. motivational interviewing

Table 1.1 Mental health Medicare items for psychologists

Mental disorder is a term used to describe a range of clinically diagnosable disorders that significantly interfere with an individual's cognitive, emotional or social abilities. This includes people with mental disorders arising from:

• chronic psychotic disorders	• drug use disorders
• acute psychotic disorders	• mixed anxiety and depression
• schizophrenia	• dissociative (conversion) disorder
• bipolar disorder	• neurasthenia
• phobic disorder	• sleep problems
• generalised anxiety disorder	• hyperkinetic (attention deficit) disorder
• adjustment disorder	• enuresis (non-organic)
• unexplained somatic complaints	• obsessive Compulsive Disorder
• depression	• mental disorder, not otherwise specified.
• sexual disorders	
• conduct disorder	
• bereavement disorder	
• post-traumatic stress disorder	
• eating disorders	
• panic disorder	
• alcohol use disorders	

3. cognitive behaviour therapy, including:

- behavioural interventions
    - behaviour modification (especially for children, including behavioural analysis and contingency management)
    - exposure techniques
    - activity scheduling
- cognitive interventions
    - cognitive analysis, challenging and restructuring
    - self-instructional training
    - attention regulation
- relaxation strategies

- guided imagery, deep muscle and isometric relaxation, controlled breathing
- skills training
- problem-solving skills training
  - anger management
  - stress management
  - communication training
  - social skills training
  - parent management training
4. interpersonal therapy (especially for depression).

There is flexibility to include narrative therapy for Aboriginal and Torres Strait Islander people.

This is a restrictive list for a general psychologist. There is no mention of schema therapy, psychoanalytic therapy, solution focused therapy, Acceptance and Commitment Therapy (ACT), hypnotherapy, Eye Movement Desensitisation and Reprocessing (EMDR), Dialectical Behaviour Therapy (DBT), Cognitive Behaviour Therapy (CBT) or Mindfulness-Based Cognitive Behaviour Therapy (MCBT). Many of these are supported by substantial evidence of effectiveness. Some therapy interventions associated with these therapies are mentioned. However, if you are considering undertaking such treatment methods, be aware that they are not sanctioned as part of the approved methods for Medicare subsidised services under Better Outcomes. The possible result, if audited, could be the payback of fees to Medicare Australia. Clinical psychologists have some greater leeway, as they are not restricted to the Focused Psychological Strategies list of interventions; however, services provided by clinical psychologists are still identified primarily as Interpersonal

Psychotherapy (IPT) and CBT according to the Medicare Australia guidelines.

Is defensive practice the answer? Defensive practice is prudent practice but it will not deliver a set of rules to practice by or bridge the gulf between theory and practice. O'Donovan, Casey, Van der Veen, and Boschen (2013) in their book, *Psychotherapy: An Australian Perspective*, emphasised risk management, the scientist-practitioner model, theoretical models and the therapeutic alliance/common factors; however, Crago (2013) in a review of the book noted:

> *Psychology emerges as hierarchical, rule governed*
> *and risk averse, valuing content over process and*
> *'technique over relationship'. (p. 70)*

If we look to what is happening on an international front, we need look no further than the situation in the United States where psychotherapy has been threatened as a viable career by the influences of 'managed care' (health insurance), 'Big Pharma' (medication marketing) and the medical model. The uptake of therapy is down and therapist incomes are low despite research that in many cases psychological therapy is more efficacious than medication. In Australia, we can heed the advice of Mary Sykes Wylie, Scott Miller, Mary Pipher, Scott Lilienfeld, Chloe Madanes, William Doherty and others who all contributed to a recent edition of *Psychotherapy Networker* (March/April 2015). In summary, the opinions of these leading psychotherapy researchers regarding real threats to the future of psychotherapy are that:

- There is a lack of a coherent description of what we do that the public can understand.

- We stubbornly cling to intuition and personal experience as guiding lights in our work rather than trusting science and research to guide us.

- We do not market the strength of the solutions we offer to human problems that has been shown to deliver superior results: empathy, goal collaboration and consensus, a professional relationship and a therapeutic method of communication with clients incorporating client feedback.

We are in a unique situation in Australia with government support for mental health treatment that other countries do not have. There are countries ahead of us, such as the Netherlands and the Scandinavian countries, but many others that are worse off. In addition, there are potentially politically difficult times ahead with the release of the 2015 Mental Health Commission *Review of Mental Health Programmes and Services* (http://www.mentalhealthcommission.gov.au), which makes a number of recommendations relevant to the (Medicare) Better Outcomes program. Those recommendations include restricting psychologists acquiring new Medicare provider numbers to practice in rural and regional Australia. Federal and state governments are always looking for ways to trim the health budget so there will probably be continuing uncertainty in relation to government funded support of private psychology services.

Summary and overview of following chapters

Private practice psychology can incorporate a range of approaches from general counselling, psychotherapy, or short-term symptom orientated interventions through to specialist services for various population groups (e.g., assessments for autism, court reports, or relationship counselling). It requires business skill and clinical acumen to build a sustainable practice. This book is a manual designed for those either entering private practice or already practising who might want to continue their professional development.

Each of the following chapters will cover different areas of private psychological practice:

- *Chapter 2.* How to set up in private practice. This chapter considers business and clinical necessities in the Australian context.

- *Chapter 3.* Compliance: Medicare audits and other regulation issues. This chapter addresses compliance with third party payers and how to comply with Psychology Board of Australia registration standards — important to survival as a private practitioner.

- *Chapter 4.* Psychological treatment in a private practice setting. This chapter explores clinical issues in a private practice setting and how to establish an effective model of service delivery.

- *Chapter 5.* Where do you belong? Consultation, supervision and professional support and self-care. This chapter encourages you to consider your networks, your professional competencies and where to find a reference point for your own professional development.

- *Chapter 6.* Ethical dilemmas in private practice land. This chapter examines clinical issues that present in private practice (and the ethical dilemmas they pose) and provides some insights and guidance as to how these may be managed.

- *Chapter 7.* Tricky and complex presentations in private practice. This chapter discusses personality disorder and comorbid presentations and how to deal with these effectively and safely in private practice.

- *Chapter 8.* Feedback informed treatment (FIT): How to and why you should implement it in private practice.

This chapter notes that effective treatment is the key to success in private practice.

- *Chapter 9.* Record keeping, case notes and writing reports. This chapter demonstrates the importance and clinical relevance of file notes, proforma assessments, and correspondence, and so on.

- *Chapter 10.* Cross-examination: Preparing for court and giving evidence. This chapter gives tips on writing reports and appearing in court.

- *Chapter 11.* Contingency planning. This chapter discusses career planning, sources of referral, professional development and diversification.

- *Chapter 12.* Closing a practice. This chapter provides advice on closing or selling your practice.

Chapter 2

How to set up in private practice

Is independent private practice right for you?

There was a time for psychologists when being in private practice was considered to be the pinnacle of success. Usually practitioners worked first in the public sector (and often for many years). This has changed. Now many graduates, straight out of university, go into independent practice. This is reflected in the changing profile of our profession (Stokes, Mathews, Grenyer, & Crea, 2010).

Of course working in the public sector has some advantages. This includes paid sick leave, annual and long service leave, career paths with an incremental classification structure, paid leave for conferences and professional development. But this is not the full story. Many practitioners crave autonomy and some measure of control over their practice.

In private practice, to paraphrase an expression, '*you eat what you kill*' — you may avoid unnecessary bureaucracy (although Medicare has its own machinations), unproductive meetings, and working to a 9 to 5 timetable. Yes, you are your own boss. In theory! The reality is that in order to be successful in private practice you need to construct a business structure that is profitable and satisfying (even if it is a business of one).

You need to know what you are good at and do it well. There are many skills you will need from the start in private practice. You must be able to tell a range of potential clients what is 'wrong' with them and be able to engage and work with them to improve in real and concrete ways.

It is also important to juggle work and other commitments. Shaw & Breckenridge (2014) presented the preliminary findings of a small qualitative research project that explored the recursive relationship between intertwining identities of 'therapist' and 'mother'. They interviewed nine therapist/mothers. The interview transcripts from their therapist sample provide instructive reading. All respondents felt that the role of therapist was important to their identity and had chosen private practice in the hope that it offered greater family flexibility. However these mothers found both necessary compromises as well as benefits. Managing home–work transitions and responsibilities was a major concern for respondents. Feeling competent as a mother and as a therapist can be difficult. It can depend on factors such as whether the person was established in their career when they had children and whether the exhaustion and sleep deprivation from having a young family impacted on their sense of their own effectiveness as a therapist.

As 78% of us are women, we must consider the juggling of work and motherhood as having many practical considerations. Independent private practice usually means that you will not receive maternity leave payments and if you don't work or can't work due to family commitments, including sick children, it will result in less income. Also there are the additional stresses of managing the expectations of your clients and your children. Work–life and family commitments can be difficult to manage despite the flexibility that private practice appears to promise. Trying to see clients in the child-free hours of 9 am to 3 pm and generate income is not straightforward — many clients will want to see you after 5 pm when they finish work. Combine this client expectation with a young family and the desire to spend time with your children and/or your partner, you may find that, rather than relaxing, you are undertaking administrative tasks related to your practice after your children go to bed. Giving to, and being present for, clients every day and then being present in your family life can take its toll.

Reflect: How are you at multi-tasking and handling emotional stress? Can you leave the work at the office? How will your partner and/or family cope with you being pre-occupied with your small business? Do they support your endeavours?

Being in business

Business 'savvy' is crucial. This requires a frank look at yourself. Do you have the ability to shift your thoughts, feelings, behaviours and goals in the direction of becoming a good business person as well as an excellent practitioner?

What if you go into practice straight from university? Or combine private practice with a part-time public sector career or raising a family? Such are the possibilities and more. But the risks don't evaporate. It is possible that suburban Australia will soon be saturated with psychologists who are working in GP clinics or multi-practitioner clinics with masseurs, physiotherapists, Reiki practitioners and the like. Medicare recognition has created an expectation from the public and GPs that psychology services will be free or bulk-billed (even if this is not financially viable for the practitioner). There are accusations from some politicians and the anti-psychologist lobby that psychologists are pork-barrelling the public purse and charging outrageous gap fees. Neither has been shown to be correct (Lindner & Stokes, 2007).

Reflect: What would you consider to be an ideal setting for your practice? Can you see yourself in that situation? How does it feel to be there?

If you see yourself in private practice, then you need to consider the following:

- *Independent private practice.* Are you at the stage of life and stage of career that independent private practice and the business model that it requires are a realistic possibility for you? Can you be at the office most days? Are you available for after-hours work?

- *Balancing business and service delivery.* Becoming a psychologist can feel like a vocation or calling but what about becoming a business person? Can you see yourself learning to love operating a business, as much as you love professional practice, with a high level of competence and integrity?

- *Practical skills.* Do you have the personal qualities, clinical acumen, appropriate life stage and robust business strategies to develop your practice in a way that will make you a success?

Other related questions that you need to answer include:

- Do I want to work from home, in a GP clinic, in a group psychology practice, in an alternative health clinic setting or in a corporate franchised setting?

- Do I want to be a contractor and be responsible for my own superannuation, leave entitlements, work-cover and professional indemnity insurances?

- Do I want to find my own clients or have them given to me?

- Do I want supervision and/or reception support as part of my package in a practice?

- Do I want to rent a room by the hour and see how I go?

- Do I want to work for a large corporatised private practice and be paid as a contractor?

- Do I want to find a salaried position in a private practice?

Some of the business models available in private practice, and their pros and cons, can be summarised as follows:

Model	Pros	Cons	Opinion
Sole practitioner working from home	Work own hours; Potentially work is family friendly; Screen referrals yourself	Isolation and safety concerns; Limited availability and access; Lack of business support; Pressure to take all/any referrals	Not advisable for those starting out in private practice; May have additional risks such as potential boundary crossings;
Sole practitioner renting rooms (e.g. GP clinic or other health clinic)	Build your own business for you	Financially tough; Isolation; Administrative load is primarily yours; Limited availability and access; Lack of business support; Pressure to take all/any referrals	May work well in combination with a public sector job;

Group practice	Peer support/ consultation and or supervision possible; Creates a greater volume of referrals; Easier to operate within your competency; Can leave work at the end of the day	You are contributing to a group practice not to your own practice; May restrict your range of work roles (e.g., primarily clinical or counselling usually); Limited autonomy; Time poor; Reliant on what is provided as part of the practice set up or have to provide yourself (e.g., tests);	Early–mid career option
Contractor with large practice with multiple sites	Peer support/ consultation and/or supervision possible; Creates a greater volume of referrals; Easier to operate within your competency; Can leave work at the end of the day	Limited autonomy, Tme poor; Reliant on what is provided as part of the practice set up or have to provide yourself (e.g., tests); You are contributing to a group practice not to your own practice; May restrict your range of work roles (e.g., primarily clinical or counselling usually); Billing choices may not be in your control	Early–mid career option

Reflect: Have you identified your practice model? Can you identify any risks associated with that model? Have you taken steps to manage any risks?

An outline of models of private practice is provided by the APS in the document *Models of private practice: A private practice guide for psychologists* (APS, 2014).

Educating the community

Lynn Grodzki (2000) identified a need for an entrepreneurial spirit in her book *Building your ideal private practice: A guide for therapists and other healing professionals.* Therapists need to think about how the general public sees therapy. She contended that therapy is not perceived as a normal part of life by anyone except therapists and daytime talk show hosts. She identified the following barriers and potential responses from therapists:

- *Therapy is weakness.* Grodzki suggested reframing our role as mentoring, taking a collaborative position, showing respect to our clients and offering ourselves as a resource rather than an expert.

- *Therapy is expensive.* We might offer a menu of therapy services for clients and refine therapy as a necessity rather than a luxury.

- *Therapy is mysterious.* We can educate the community through websites, free workshops etc.

Other psychologists have gone a step further. The Colorado Centre for Clinical Excellence doesn't just cite studies supporting the effectiveness of therapy and counselling, they actually publish the results of each of their therapists (see www.thecolaradocenter.com) on a treatment effectiveness or outcome measure, the Outcome Rating Scale (ORS), and provide graphs of their results versus industry averages. They note on their website 'we specialise in a variety of well-established effective methods not fads'. They seek to differentiate themselves from the other practices around them and to show their level of effectiveness with their clients as a way of legitimately promoting their practice. Australian psychologist, Dr Aaron Frost has attempted something similar in his website (www.benchmarkpsychology.com.au) where he demonstrates the effectiveness of regular use of outcome measures by gathering data of the seven psychologists in his practice and calculating their statistical effect size (usually a comparison of the magnitude of change attributable to treatment by comparing a treated sample to an untreated sample) of each clinician's clients as a group. He contends that with this approach clinicians can detect clients who are at risk of dropout, not progressing or getting worse and adjust the therapy process accordingly.

> Reflect: If you saw yourself as more like a psychological coach than a mental health clinician, what difference would that make to your practice?

Whatever the model of business you adopt, there is still the question of how you practice. All psychologists are trained in the scientist-practitioner model but some forget the 'scientist' part after they leave university. The therapeutic conversation begins with 'How has your week/fortnight been?' Sometimes the idea of testing is limited to administering a self-report measure such as the Depression Anxiety and Stress Scale (DASS). The full range of techniques and models is neglected. The 'science-lite' practitioner will not use personality tests, health tests, projective tests, self-report questionnaires or routinely administer outcome measures despite the evidence that feedback informed treatment enhances the therapeutic alliance and promotes therapeutic change. It is hard to avoid the conclusion that such practitioners short change the profession and their clients.

Practicalities

If you are setting up a private practice then you will need to think about issues such as:

- *Files.* Where will I keep them? Will they be paper or electronic or a combination of the two? What note taking approach do I want to be my standard?

- *Outcome Measures.* Do I intend to routinely administer outcome measures and how will I integrate this into my approach?

- *Tests.* What tests would be best to purchase in the first instance and what should I budget for in terms of a professional library and test library over time?

- *Professional Development.* How will I determine a reasonable continuing professional development (CPD) budget and how do I develop a learning plan that will facilitate my business and clinical development goals? How will I fund the expenses incurred in attending professional workshops?

- *Ethical and Legal Considerations.* Where will you source advice from more experienced practitioners to common practice questions such as 'Should I keep the confidences of a 15 year old client?' or 'A client's solicitor has called me. What are my obligations?' or 'I have been asked to write a report for a client. How do I decide what to include?'.

Initial outlay

So what will you need for your practice apart from a room with furniture? You should consider the location of your practice. Think about how easy it is for clients to get to you, including public transport options and the availability of parking for those who drive. You will need to consider how close you are to possible referrers, and your competencies and passions in regards client type and therapy type. In terms of assessment, you should consider setting up a test and professional resources library for yourself over time. It would be advisable if you are undertaking general clinical/counselling practice to think about test acquisitions as your budget allows.

Test library options

Test category	Options
General mental health	Depression Anxiety Stress Scale (DASS; Lovibond & Lovibond, 1995)
	Beck Depression Inventory (BDI; Beck, Steer, & Brown, 1996)
	Beck Anxiety Inventory (BAI; Beck & Steer, 1993)
	Strengths and Difficulties Questionnaire (SDQ; Goodman, 1997)
Health and chronic illness	Pain Questionnaires (e.g. The Chronic Pain Coping Inventory, CPCI; Jensen, Turner, Romano, & Strom, 1995)
	Eating Disorder Inventory (EDI 3; Garner, 2004)
Trauma	Trauma Symptom Inventory (TSI-2; Briere, 1995)
	Post-Traumatic Stress Disorder Checklist (PCL; Weathers, Litz, Herman, Huska, & Keane, 1993)
Psychopathology	Minnesota Multiphasic Personality Inventory (MMPI-2; Butcher, Dahlstrom, Graham, Tellegen, & Kreammer, 1989)
	Minnesota Multiphasic Personality Inventory Restructured Form (MMPI-RF; Ben-Porath & Tellegen, 2011)
	Personality Assessment Inventory (PAI; Morey, 2007)
	Millon Clinical Multiaxial Inventory (MCMI-III; Millon, Milon, Davis & Grossman, 2009)

Personality	Sixteen Personality Factor Questionnaire (16PF; Russell & Karol, 2002)
	Young Schema Questionnaire Version 3 (YSQ; Young & Brown, 1994)
	Schema Mode Inventory (SMI v.1; Young et al., 2007)
Projective tests	Pictured Feelings Instrument (PFI; Stone, 2004)
Career testing	Motivated Skills Card Sort (Knowdell, 2002b)
	Occupational Interests Card Sort (Knowdell, 2002c)
	Career Values Card Sort (Knowdell, 2002a)
	Self-Directed Search (SDS; Holland, 1994)
Feedback tools (Feedback Informed Treatment)	Outcome Rating Scale (ORS; Miller & Bargmann, 2012)
	The Session Rating Scale (SRS; Miller & Bargmann, 2012)

Other resources

Other important tools are CDs for meditation (e.g., a free download from Canberra Clinical and Forensic Psychology website (www.ccfpsych.com.au), downloads, St Luke's resources such as the strength cards (available from St Luke's Innovative Resources — www.innovativeresources.org). Also consider Acceptance and Commitment Therapy (ACT) and other educational handouts (available from Dr Russ Harris' website — www.actmadesimple.com).

You may wish to consider options such as computer-based administration of tests. This is an option offered by a number of test distributors. You will need to consider the cost of tests and other resources that you may find useful or wish to lend to clients (e.g., mindfulness CDs, books on anxiety and depression or other high prevalence disorders). There are many sites on the web where you can acquire great handouts and client resources. A recent book by John Norcross (2013) *Self-help that works: Resources to improve emotional health and strengthen relationships* is worth considering. This books details self-help books, films, internet sites, online programs, online support groups and autobiographies that may be of assistance to clients. It has its drawbacks as it was written for a USA audience but is nonetheless a comprehensive encyclopaedia of self-help resources.

Digital applications are another way of procuring tests that can be administered on various devices (e.g., iPads, tablets or computers). These are becoming more and more sophisticated and cost-effective for practitioners and clients alike. There are apps such as 'Novopsych' that combine common screening tests such as the K10 and the DASS that you can buy and utilise on a number of devices as required. Often digitally presented testing is quicker (given that most of the apps score the test and provide a report on the client's results) and more motivating for the client than a paper and pen version of the same test which the psychologist then has to score after the session.

Note: There is an excellent online source of tests and automatic scoring at PARIconnect (www.pariconnect.com). You pay for what you use and the list of tests, which includes PAI and many other tests, is constantly being added to.

Most psychology practices have websites and some use practice management systems that allow for online bookings or at least email enquiries for appointments and referrals. Online bookings may be useful for practitioners renting rooms without administrative support but can have the drawback of not allowing for any screening of new clients. Websites are not necessarily expensive to develop but need to be professional and comply with advertising guidelines devised by the Psychology Board of Australia,[1] including avoiding testimonials and claims of being able to cure all ills! (www.psychologyboard.gov.au).

Other initial outlays may include a database and invoicing system (see the APS review of practice management tools) and you will need to factor in ongoing fixed and variable costs for your practice. You will need to consider how many referrals convert to clients presenting for first appointments and following through the treatment plan that you construct with them. For example 80% conversion of enquiry to attendance at a first appointment may be a reasonable goal.

Time is money

As a guide, we suggest that you consider how many hours of billable time you need to achieve each week to cover fixed and

Monthly profit/Loss scenario

Assumptions	Billable Clients	Non-billable but	Other adminis-	Fixed and
38 hr week	per 5 day week	client related	tration/marketing	variable costs
Working 48 wks per year including CPD hours	@ average of 5 per day @ 1–2 bulk bill clients per day	work @ 2 hrs per day (e.g., reports)	Following up bad debts	per month
CPD = 30 hrs per year		GP follow-ups	Preparing and lodging BAS	
Supervision/peer consultation = 1.5 hrs per month		Letters to referrers	Invoicing	
		Test administration	Medicare follow ups	
	BB = $85 X 20 hrs = $1700	Non-billable hrs = 40 hrs		Rent
	Full fee paying @$150 per sessions x 80 hrs = $12000	(Sounds like a lot but is necessary!)		Utilities
				Tests
				Admin fees
				Stationery
				Computer
				Postage
				Phone call costs
				Insurance costs

		Association and registration fees
		Library
		Tax
		GST recoup
		Data base (e.g., MYOB or psychology specific system incorporating client details)
Total potential income = $2900	Nil income	All of the above to be covered by the practitioner
60% = $1740		40% of fees earned = (approx.) $1160

variable costs and pay yourself at least 60% of the fees earned. The following table is an example of a monthly profit and loss scenario for a registered psychologist (not clinically endorsed).

Minimalist models

There are many psychologists operating what might be called a 'minimal standard business model'. They conduct their business/practice via a mobile phone, make their appointments and administer their own billing. This approach is somewhat fraught with ethical and risk management dilemmas. It is easy to be 'swamped' with work treating 6 to 8 clients per day, preparing for sessions, writing up files and letters to referrers. Then you need to find time to return calls to potential clients and make appointments. You may find there are not enough hours in the day. Self-care can easily suffer. You may soon lose clients who do not hear from you within a reasonable time period. Many will go to another psychologist, referrers may find it difficult to get in touch with you and there will be a sense of increasing pressure on you to work longer and harder. This is where mistakes can be made and complaints arise.

Reflect: Evaluate your current and future plans and obtain advice from a range of experts such as an accountant, commercial lawyer, and a senior psychologist colleague or supervisor.

Joining a group practice

If you decide to join an existing group practice, you may want to consider whether their business model and approach to psychological practice are consistent with your ethics and professional values. Does the group practice have policies regarding managing ethical obligations (e.g., the management of treating multiple family members, informed consent policies, fee structure policies)? What if a family member is paying for the treatment of another family member — what is the group practices' policy regarding confidentiality? Does the practice expect you to keep seeing clients regardless of the efficacy of treatment thus promoting client dependency? Does the group practice have a health records policy and protocols for note keeping, informed consent and financial transparency? (Barnett, Zimmerman, & Walfish, 2014)

With regards to business models, you will need to obtain advice and consider the group practice approach to fees and cost sharing and other matters. Is the group practice offering for you to join on a contractor basis/'mixed model' (e.g., where the psychologist pays a percentage of the client fee to the principal of the group practice who supplies administration support and clients but does not cover taxation, superannuation or workers compensation obligations)? Is the group practice your employer and you are a PAYE employee?

Are you renting rooms from the principal and taking care of all of your expenses/billing and referrals yourself?

Many business arrangements are formulated to maximise the take-home fee for the practitioner. Unfortunately the issue of taxation, workers compensation and superannuation coverage is sometimes left unspoken between the contractor and the principal of the practice. Risks associated with this approach include:

- Are you able to make ongoing regular payments into your superannuation fund? Many contractor arrangements do not include superannuation payments to contractors' funds. This is assumed to be the contractor's responsibility.

- Are you considered an 'employee' for the purposes of Workers Compensation insurance schemes? If the practice contracting you does not pay workers compensation premiums on your behalf and you are injured, then you may find yourself in conflict with the practice regarding loss of wages and medical expenses etc.

- Are you able to take care of your taxation responsibilities? Again, many contractor arrangements assume that the contractor will take care of their own taxation payments each financial year.

> Reflect: There is a common practice among psychologists of joining a group practice and paying the established psychologist a percentage of fees, up to 50% or more. We think that this raises some ethical concerns because the practice may be profiting by a referral to an individual practitioner. Think about this before you agree and discuss with your clinical supervisor or peer supervision group.

Summary

Do you go into independent practice? Have you developed a business 'savvy'? Do you have a context for practice that suits your development as a practitioner? These important questions and others have been raised in this chapter. It is also important to have practice resources including psychological tests and to not forget the scientist part of the scientist-practitioner model.

Chapter 3

Compliance: Medicare audits and other regulation issues

Self-care and compliance — these may appear to be unlikely 'bedfellows' but they are essential to a healthy practice. The practitioner needs to be able to sleep at night and function during the day!

In this chapter the issue of compliance will be addressed in relation to regulations and regulators. We will then begin to emphasise the importance of emotional self-care. Both are essential in knowing how to look after yourself in the challenging world of private practice.

Compliance is for your sake and that of your clients

Compliance is variously described as the way in which the state maintains order such as '*compliance* (our italics) with the Clinical Framework' for WorkSafe Victoria (Health Services Group, 2012), and 'the primary aim of a *compliance* (our italics) audit is to verify that both the provider and the client were eligible for Medicare benefits and that the services provided met all Medicare requirements' from Medicare Australia (Mathews, 2011). These ideas of compliance can lead to different reactions in practitioners. Demands for compliance can create fear and avoidance or a sense of entitlement and rebellion or apathy and disinterest in practitioners. None of these responses are likely to be adaptive if you want to stay in business as a psychologist.

In an issue of *InPsych*, Rebecca Mathews (2014) noted that the PsyBA has announced random audits of psychologists to check if they meet the registration standards for:

- continuing professional development (CPD)
- professional indemnity insurance (PII)
- criminal history
- recency of practice.

But what does that mean for you? It means that you need to comply with the legislation and National Board policies regarding these standards. With CPD you need to be able to show that you have a learning plan and evidence of CPD attendance with documented journaling. With PII, you need to show that you have cover that is aligned with your work and covers the minimum requirements. Criminal history and recency of practice have their own definitions and you should refer to these on the PsyBA website (http://www.psychology-board.gov.au).

Audits by other regulators (e.g., Primary Health Networks or other bodies who are administering Access to Allied Psychological Services (ATAPS) for Medicare Australia or workers compensation schemes) usually require evidence of attendance, treatment undertaken, compliance with standards such as Working with Children Check (WCC), PII, and registration standards as a minimum. They want to see that your files and note taking are organised and not a pile of papers floating around in a folder. If stationery and organisation of files is not your strength then utilise a practice manager or professional assistant as a disorganised file will tend to invite unwelcome interest from the auditor.

Mathews (2011) also noted that Medicare reviews individual health providers 'whose billing patterns are different from their peers and may indicate inappropriate practice'. A recent book published by Tony Pastore (2013), *The anxiety of psychological practice in Australia: Surviving in private practice*, detailed his travails through billing reviews by WorkCover, audits by Medicare Australia and subsequent complaints to the Australian Health Practitioner Regulation Agency (AHPRA). His final edict is 'protect yourself with good, sound practices and good, sound records to prove your innocence' (p. 67).

Key learning point

- Measurement of treatment outcomes over time and clear and precise record keeping will go a long way towards addressing audits or reviews by third party payers (e.g., Medicare Australia, workers compensation schemes, victims of crime tribunals). Review both outcome measures that are symptom focused as well as those that measure progress (functional outcome measures) in treatment. Become familiar with which type of outcome measure should be utilised when and with which type of clients.

In order to remain sane and solvent, it is important to remember the following:

- Do not begin treating a client without the paperwork required (e.g., Mental Health Treatment plan and/or GP referral). If you are undertaking Medicare eligible work you must comply with their expectations or risk repayment of fees on audit.

- Do not see clients unless the paperwork for ongoing treatment is in order. Make sure a review letter has been received by you prior to the seventh session for Better Outcomes or Medicare funded counselling. Auditors consider post-dating as fraud that may attract sanctions. Do not 'forget' to send a discharge letter, preferably with a K10 score, to the GP at the conclusion of either 10 sessions or the treatment plan.

- The psychological treatment must be compliant with the parameters of the program funding it. Workers compensation systems fund psychological treatment related to a work injury. This does not include counselling related to childhood sexual abuse, marital counselling or family therapy. Prior approval for psychological treatment is advisable with all third party payers — in writing.

To paraphrase Medicare Australia, the purpose of a compliance audit is to verify that both the provider and the client are eligible for benefits and that the services provided meet all Medicare requirements[1] (see http://www.humanservices.gov.au). Auditing can target various parameters including unusual service patterns. Audits can cover claims up to two years previously, up to 20 clients (and their files), and billing. Access to records is supported by Medicare legislation. The Australian Psychological Society (APS) provides support to psychologists for compliance with Medicare auditing[2] (see http://www.psychology.org.au). Primarily the audits will review referral requirements (e.g., letters provided at the appropriate points in a treatment episode of up to 10 sessions in a calendar year), billing requirements (e.g., use of appropriate item codes, evidence that you saw the client on the dates billed, evidence of service time that was billed and evidence of out-of-office sessions if being claimed).

It is in the interests of all Medicare providers to compare their billing to others as one method of examining whether your billing patterns would identify you as an outlier[3] (see www.medicareaustralia.gov.au).

Compensation schemes also have billing review or compliance programs and can review payments for services made to their claimants. In most schemes, the insurers will be obliged

---

1 http://www.humanservices.gov.au/corporate/publications-and-resources/compliance-program
2 http://www.psychology.org.au/medicare
3 www.medicareaustralia.gov.au/about/stats/provider-percentile-charts.jsp

to formally notify you that they are requesting patient health information under a particular legislative provision. You may request that files are reviewed by psychologists only. Compensations schemes are obliged to comply with privacy and health records legislation in all jurisdictions when accessing patient information. The compensation schemes can consider whether the treatment you provided to a claimant is clinically justified, whether payments made for services comply with their policies and whether your client files are adequate. Outcomes from such reviews can include requests for further information, reimbursement of inappropriate payments, and/or referral to AHPRA regarding poor performance or possible professional misconduct.

Reflect: Think about a practice audit. This would include any risk factors that might lead to complaints. Who would you ask to help you? Could you agree to help them as well? This might be discussed in supervision.

Author comment

Kaye: I have been the supervisor for psychologists who have been audited by WorkCover in Victoria or had complaints and required mandated supervision under AHPRA and the PsyBA. In all cases, they were psychologists who had lost sight of the standards required of them. They were not bad people and usually they were good psychologists but they had bad habits. They lacked self-care and were disconnected from their peers and colleagues. Usually they did not understand current practice requirements. In some cases they had let their practice dwindle down to a predictable and narrow repertoire of interventions. Case notes were poor or illegible. Their client files did not contain basic client information, informed consents, details of treat-

ment plans and progress against treatment goals. They were tired, burnt out and insular. They were working long hours and seeing too many clients per day. They had personal problems that distracted them from their work and they had not reviewed their work context in response to their personal difficulties.

Positive behaviours for self-care

Elizabeth Shaw (2014) writing on burn-out said:

> It is tempting on the return to work to make the same old resolutions about getting more home/work balance … Our work does take a different toll but we have to be realistic about how this is managed. The breaks we need to avoid are, of course, those provided by denial, grandiosity and substance abuse. (p. 65)

Reflect: Do you have an intake system that screens for emotional load on yourself? Do you regularly review your fees, your work practices, your filing and documentation, and your business practices? Do you have a timetable that allows you to easily put your hand on any requirement that might be requested by an auditor? Have you discussed all this with your supervisor or peer supervision group?

To Do:

Undertake the Professional Practice Management Standards Self-Assessment (APS) online. If you are considering setting up a private practice consider undertaking the APS online course Fundamentals of Private Practice (eight self-paced modules that will take 10–15 hours to complete) as part of your CPD learning plan for the year.

Summary

We practice with a measure of professional privilege. This comes with a range of expectations from a number of sources. There are, of course, short-cuts but they easily become regrets. Decide to be cautious and highly aware of issues of compliance.

Chapter 4

Psychological treatment in a private practice setting

Proven strategies for therapeutic success

Just what works? This question was addressed in a recent article 'Compendium of treatment adaptations' that summarised meta-analytic research about adapting psychotherapy to individual clients (Norcross & Lambert, 2013). There were six trans-diagnostic features: reactance level (compliance-defiance continuum), stages of change, preference for treatment modality (e.g., psychotherapy vs medication), therapy method (including Cognitive-Behaviour Therapy [CBT] and acceptance and commitment therapy [ACT]), therapist characteristics (such as gender) and treatment length. The following is a brief summary of the findings:

- *Systematically vary your directness.* Do this with the client to enhance treatment results and to decrease dropouts.

- *Methods.* Psycho-education and emotion generating counselling methods work best for clients contemplating change while skills training and behavioural methods work best for those who are in the action stage.

- **Client preferences.** An intake or first session review that recognises and accommodates the preferences of clients. This will include treatment method, therapist characteristics and treatment length. Doing this is likely to reduce barriers to treatment.

- **Coping style.** The client's predominant coping style (blame themselves 'internalisers', act out 'externalisers', for example) should be matched to the focus of treatment so as to enhance treatment outcome: internalising clients tend to find interpersonal and insight-orientated treatments more effective while symptom-focused and skill building treatment tend to be more effective among externalising clients.

- **Overall.** The outcome research suggests that reducing symptoms and stabilising clients initially, then switching to more indirect or insight-oriented approaches, is likely to be effective with most clients.

Think about the following clients in light of this research. How would you approach treatment?

Mary is depressed following a separation from her fiancé. She said, 'I really hoped this relationship would work. But I have a 'poor track record'. I am not sure what I am doing wrong. I know I need help to change how I relate to men.'

Barry is court referred for treatment. He has had a number of convictions related to driving while intoxicated and other offences. He wants to avoid going to prison and attending treatment will give him 'another chance'. He seemed doubtful that counselling could be 'much help'.

Reflect: You might consider outlining a treatment plan for both. What is similar? What is different? Do you have a pro-forma assessment that allows you to gather all of the required information to create a collaborative treatment plan?

Treatment options

Author comment

Kaye: It never fails to amaze me in supervising many therapists and psychologists, who have undertaken 6 to 8 years of training, that many do not routinely administer standardised tests, develop and document clinical formulations, have little ability to take comprehensive contemporaneous notes and do not have treatment plans or assessments documented and shared with their clients.

So what are the reasons for this phenomenon? Perhaps most of these supervisees have had placements and access to test libraries during their training. However, when they enter private practice these resources are unavailable. This might be due to cost or the particular business model of the practice they have joined. Perhaps expectations change and standards are compromised. Lack of structure and an external expectation of meeting a certain standard in order to pass a subject or placement when in training can lead to sloppy methods and corner cutting.

This can become a recipe for disaster. You may find yourself practicing at a lower standard, without putting into practice your professional training and thereby disadvantaging your clients. You end up selling yourself and your clients short. The table below describes one way of thinking about different types of presentations in private practice. As you can see, the presentations are divided into three 'levels'. Regardless of the (arbitrary) level that any one client may typify, psychologists are encouraged to consider undertaking relevant assessments (including testing), developing a clinical formulation and treatment planning and eliciting client feedback on a regular basis to encourage clients to collaborate in their therapy goals with the therapist and to minimise treatment dropout.

For any presentation, the therapist must therefore adapt his or her treatment style, use of self, therapy methods and feedback and review approach. Each of the levels of presentation includes and builds upon the previous level, adding further elements of complexity (apart from Level 1, which stands alone).

For each of the three levels of client presentation and their corollary treatment methods, outcome measures, self-report questionnaires and other tests are outlined in the table below:

Table of Levels of Client Presentation and Associated Elements of Assessment and Treatment

Level 1

Type of presentation	Outcome measures	Self-report question-naires	Other tests, homework exercises	Treatment modalities	Optimal length of therapy
Symptom reduction (e.g., anxiety, depression, stress)	Outcome Rating Scale (ORS) Session Rating Scale (SRS)	For example Depression Anxiety Stress Scale (DASS)Beck inventories (Beck Depression Inventory BDI/Beck Anxiety Inventory BAI)	Happiness Trap www.psychologytools.org www.cci.health.wa.gov.au	For example Cognitive Behaviour Therapy (CBT; Beck, 2011) Mindfulness-Based Cognitive Therapy (MBCT; Segal, Williams, & Teasdale, 2002) Acceptance and Commitment Therapy (ACT; Hayes, Strosahl, & Wilson, 1999) Solution focused therapy (SFBT; de Shazer et al., 2007) Interpersonal Psychotherapy (IPT; Weissman, Markowitz, & Klerman, 2007)	5–10 sessions

Level 2

Type of presentation	Outcome measures	Self-report question-naires	Other tests	Treatment modalities	Optimal length of therapy
Level 1+ complexity in the form of co-morbidities+characterological or personality structure issues	ORS/SRS Test/re-test Baseline measures	As above plus Young Schema Questionnaire (YSQ) Eating Disorders Inventory (EDI3) Chronic Pain Coping Inventory (CPCI) Pictured Feelings Instrument Card Sorts Cognitive testing	For example Sixteen Personality Factor Questionnaire (16PF) Neuroticism, Extraversion, Openness Personality Inventory Revised (NEO-PI-R) Personality Assessment Inventory (PAI) California Psychological Inventory (CPI)	As above plus For example Schema Therapy (Young, Klosko, & Weishaar, 2003) Emotionally Focused Therapies (EFT; Elliot, Goldman, & Greenberg, 2004) Psychodynamic therapies (Cabaniss, 2011)Summers & Baraber (2010)	10+ sessions

Level 3

Type of presentation	Outcome measures	Self-report question-naires	Other tests	Treatment modalities	Optimal length of therapy
Level 1+2+ Complex co-morbidities plus trauma (past and/or current) plus involvement with third party issues (e.g., compensation schemes, legal action plus failed treatment previously)	As above	As above plus For example Trauma Symptom Inventory (TSI)	Minnesota Multiphasic Personality inventory (MMPI2/MMPI 2-RF)	As above Eye Movement Desensitization and Reprocessing (EMDR; Shapiro, 2001) Hypnotherapy (Burrows, Stanley, & Bloom, 2001) Projective methods Psychodynamic methods (Cabaniss, 2011) Virtual Reality Therapy (North, North, & Coble, 1996) Schema therapy (Young, Klosko, & Weishaar., 2003) Arntz & Jacob (2013)	10+ sessions

The following case examples further illustrates the three levels
of presentation:

Case Example

Level 1

Matthew is a 38-year-old married man with three young children.
He has a history of anxiety and some depressive episodes but has
not sought treatment previously. He attended his GP complaining
of being irritable with his wife and kids, early waking and restless
sleep, low sex drive, stressful work deadlines and weight gain over
the last six months. Matthew's GP diagnosed him as suffering
from an Adjustment Disorder with Mixed Anxiety and Depressed
Mood. Matthew stated that he generally recovers from these
episodes without external help and tends to increase his exercise
levels (he is a keen jogger and bike rider) to cope with his
problems. Assessment could involve administering the Depression,
Anxiety and Stress Scales (DASS), the Outcome Rating Scale
(ORS) and or other symptom self-report measures. Therapy could
involve Cognitive Behaviour Therapy (CBT), Acceptance and
Commitment Therapy (ACT), Mindfulness-Based Cognitive
Behavioural Therapy (MCBT). Interventions could involve cognitive methods such as cognitive re-structuring, thought dairies
ABC (RET) analysis of thoughts, feelings and disputation
methods, or mindfulness, ACT exercises, relaxation training,
activity scheduling etc.

Level 2

Matthew is a 38-year-old married man with three young children.
He has a history of anxiety and some depressive episodes but has
not sought treatment previously. He attended his GP complaining
of being irritable with his wife and kids, early waking and restless
sleep, low sex drive, stressful work deadlines and weight gain over
the last six months. He reported that he and his wife had recently
invested in a small business together that she was going to operate
and along with their mortgage on their house were now finan-

cially 'under pressure'. Their youngest child who is 5 years old has been recently diagnosed with Autism Spectrum Disorder (ASD). Matthew stated that he found his son hard to bond with and tended to leave him to his wife to handle. He believed this was creating marital tensions between them. Matthew reported that he has also been drinking a bottle of wine per night regularly for about six months and occasionally uses cannabis with friends to relax. Matthew's GP diagnosed him as suffering from an Adjustment Disorder with Mixed Anxiety and Depressed Mood. Assessment could involve the DASS, the ORS and/other symptom self-report measures. Other measures could include the 16 Personality Factor Questionnaire (16 PF), Neuroticism, Extraversion, Openness Personality Inventory (NEO PI-R), Minnesota Multiphasic Personality Inventory (MMPI2) or Young Schema Questionnaire (YSQ-3) to understand characterological or personality issues, and/or self-report measures of substance use (e.g., Turning Point online self-assessment). Therapy could involve CBT, ACT, MCBT, Cognitive Analytic Therapy (CAT; Ryle & Kerr, 2002), Evidence-Based Psychodynamic1 Therapy, Schema Therapy, Emotion-Focused Therapy. Interventions could involve cognitive and behavioural methods, depth psychology methods, identification of patterns from Family of Origin, harm minimisation techniques, referral to a drug and alcohol physician or service, marital therapy techniques (or referral to couple therapist).

Level 3

Matthew is a 38-year-old married man with three young children. He has a history of anxiety and some depressive episodes and has sought treatment previously — six sessions with another psychologist 6 months ago. He did not find 'just talking' very helpful. He attended his GP complaining of being irritable with his wife and kids, early waking and restless sleep, low sex drive, stressful work deadlines and weight gain over the last six months. He reported that he and his wife had recently invested in a small business together that she was going to operate and along with their mortgage on their house were now financially 'under pressure'. He had obtained the money to invest in the business via a compensation claim regarding a physical work injury (back injury) he suffered 3 years ago. His youngest child, who is 5 years old, has been recently diagnosed with ASD. Matthew stated that he found his son hard to bond with and tended to leave him to his wife to handle. He believed this was creating marital tensions between them. Matthew reported that he has also been drinking a bottle of wine per night regularly for about six months and occasionally uses cannabis with friends to relax. Matthew's GP diagnosed him as suffering from an Adjustment Disorder with Mixed Anxiety and Depressed Mood. Assessment could involve the DASS, the ORS and/other symptom self-report measures. Other measures could 16 PF, NEO, MMPI2, YSQ-3 to understand characterological or personality issues, and/or self-report measures of substance use (e.g., Turning Point online self-assessment1). Therapy could involve CBT, ACT, MCBT, CAT, Evidence-based Psychodynamic Therapy, Schema Therapy, Emotion-Focused Therapy. Interventions could involve cognitive and behavioural methods, depth psychology methods, identification of patterns from Family of Origin, harm minimisation techniques, referral to a drug and alcohol physician or service, marital therapy techniques (or referral to couple therapist) and/or family therapy. He may require assistance with chronic pain from his work injury that could include hypnotherapy, psychological pain management techniques or referral to a multidisciplinary team for assessment and treatment of the chronic pain. Matthew asked that his treatment be covered by his workers compensation claim so this would need to be approved and a treatment plan outlined with outcome measures.

Key learning points

- Regularly share with the client where you think the therapy is and jointly evaluate progress.

- Return to the original goals and honour the position the client has taken rather than acting like a disapproving parent.

- Use straight-forward direct language when challenging a client and wait for change rather than pushing it.

---

1 http://www.turningpoint.org.au/Treatment/Online-Self-Assessment.aspx

Treatment planning

A treatment plan is only of value if it is used as a guide for each session and is an overall framework for the psychological services provided to a client. There are many models of treatment planning but they commonly include:

- A statement as to the presenting problems or difficulties of the client.

- An analysis of the context and history of these problems. For example, the 'Four Ps' is a simple method of noting various factors — predisposing factors, precipitating factors, perpetuating factors and perpetuating factors (Weerasekera, 1996).

- Case formulation or conceptualisation that is a set of hypotheses that link the data collected with underlying dynamics of a client so as to inform the treatment plan rather than reiterating the client's narrative of their situation.

- Goals that preferably allow for the client's voice to be heard and are written with the client's view and stated reason for presenting for treatment in mind.

- Psychometric assessments — this would include a list of standardised tests (including functional outcome and therapeutic alliance measures), symptom measures as well as tests of psychopathology or personality.

- Interventions and homework/handouts — these would be listed and should include (but are not necessarily limited to) Focussed Psychological Strategies (FPS) and other interventions or homework/handouts given to the clients.

Other optional categories of data that could be included depending on your therapeutic orientation could be core beliefs, automatic thoughts, compensatory strategies or coping strategies. A treatment plan is not an assessment document. Assessment documentation can include family of origin information in detail and other personal information regarding the client that you would like to record.

> To Read: Pearl Berman (2014). *Case conceptualization and treatment planning: Integrating theory with clinical practice.* This excellent book will help in this important task.

To Do:

When you think through your treatment plan carefully consider the sequence of interventions. One example is Behavioural Activation early in the treatment of depression to provide a lift in mood to raise the chances that homework tasks such as a thought diary might be completed.

In terms of your clinical file for a client, it might be useful to utilise a one-page treatment summary similar to this proforma document on the page opposite (page 51).

Technological tips in private practice

Digital technology has much to offer the time-poor psychologist in private practice. Handheld tablet devices can be used for digital administration of frequently used psychometrics via apps. Apps in general are helpful to monitor mood, practice strategies, and assist clients to motivate themselves. Apps can be the basis for homework exercises and provide means to record progress outside sessions or practice certain skills such as mindfulness. It is also possible to purchase apps that allow for the digital administration of frequently utilised measures such as the DASS 21 and the K10 and storage of data

Table 4.1 Example of a Treatment Plan Summary

TREATMENT PLAN SUMMARY

CLIENT NAME: _____

Presenting Problems

_____

Predisposing Factors

_____

Precipitating Factors

_____

Protective Factors

_____

Perpetuating Factors

_____

Clinical Formulation/Diagnosis

_____

Interventions Summary

_____

What does the client want? (stated goal)

In what way does he/she hope to achieve the goal(s)? (the means)

Consistent with what values and preferences? (client preferences)

What is the therapist's role in the process? (relationship)

GOALS

1.

2.

3.

_____

Handouts	ORS/SRS	YES/NO
Other Tests		

---

from these administrations. Some apps that we have found helpful in everyday practice and some that have been recommended by clients and can be purchased from iTunes are:

- *Moodkit*: For monitoring mood and activity scheduling
- *Autism Apps*: A listing of all autism and ASD apps that may be useful for therapy with this client group
- *Novopsych:* There are15 different tests on one app including K10, DASS, Impact of Events Scale, Zung Depression test
- *iCBt:* self-paced CBT monitoring program
- *Love Maps* (Gottman app): Facilitation questions for couples wanting to improve communication
- *ACT Happiness Trap App:* This app offers Acceptance and Commitment Therapy exercises and strategies.

Where do you belong? Consultation, supervision and professional support and self-care

The old real estate mantra is 'position, position, position'. How do you rate yourself in the following areas?

Professional support and self-care

It is easy to become overwhelmed as a practitioner. Demands come from every aspect of our professional and private lives. Andrew May (2007) in his book, *Flip the switch,* identified 10 'overload demons'. Ask yourself if you:

1. Always make yourself available?

2. Find it hard saying no (colloquially known as the 'Noddy Syndrome')?

3. Spend half the day responding to emails?

4. Feel totally controlled by the clock?

5. Think information overload is your middle name?

6. Feel like you're running from appointment to appointment, crisis to crisis?

7. Are too busy to eat properly, take time out, socialise, or make it to your children's athletics carnival?

8. Spend half your holidays sick or recovering from work-related stress?

9. Take your mobile or laptop with you on holidays?

10. Feel burnt out?

> *Author comment*
>
> *Kaye: I know that some if not all of these issues have applied to me at various times in my career. It is amazing how readily we dole out advice to our clients that we are often reluctant or unlikely to take ourselves. It is interesting to reflect on how little we apply the principles and practices of CBT to our own negative thinking, practice mindfulness or positive psychology or relationship enhancement techniques to our own sorry lives! On top of this, in the private practice world there is often no one and nothing standing between you and your own foibles and downfalls. There is no P3 senior psychologist or job description or time clock that specifies when you clock on and when you clock off. It is up to you.*

The Psychologists Board of Victoria in their 2009 publication *Health Matters for Psychologists* divided up self-care into three domains:

- managing pressures on yourself as a psychologist
- alleviating stress and preventing professional impairment
- maintaining good health.

Each of these will be broken into subsections, including some questions or issues to consider in regards each:

Managing pressures as a psychologist

How do you know you are successful in private practice?
Create feedback mechanisms that identify your successes and areas in which you can improve.

Isolation and confidentiality — who do you talk to about your work?

Compassion Fatigue: overloaded with a client's distress and tragedies.

Personal issues and life events — if a critical life situation happens to you, what do you do to ensure continuing competency in your work?

Alleviating stress and preventing professional impairment

How do you maintain work–life balance?

Managing stress differently dependent upon the stage you are in your career: early career = motivated but anxious/uncertain; mid-career = juggling competing personal and work interests; late career = keeping up with your profession while looking for a change of pace. Identify where you are in this continuum and reflect on the challenges presented.

Impairment — what if you see it in a colleague? What if you are impaired yourself?

Maintaining good health

Less self-diagnosis and self-prescribing or self-medicating and more independent evaluation of your health on a regular basis is a solid foundation for general good health.

Mental health issues — seek independent advice on your mental health, consult peers about how you are travelling and think about personal therapy.

Personal care strategies: Is your exercise, diet and stress reduction regime sustainable and consistent?

What is your optimum workload? How are you monitoring your workload and therapeutic efficacy?

Set personal and professional boundaries at work — eat regularly, take breaks and limit complex cases and client consultations each day.

Find debriefing opportunities, ways of being in regular contact with colleagues, and supervision and consultation.

Make sure the environment you are working in is comfortable and you feel a sense of purpose when you are in that space.

Prevent burnout — maintain connection with our profession through CPD and acknowledge when your workload needs adjusting up or down. Take regular leave and plan this for the year ahead if possible.

The quest for a supervisor or mentor

We are never 'self-sufficient' in practice. We need other colleagues to sustain us in the work that we do. The ideal is not the *sole* practitioner, but a person practicing within a community of supportive relationships.

How do we foster our own excellence and mastery? Finding the right supervisor(s) and/or mentor(s) is a good starting point to reduce isolation and to enhance competence and professional development. Michael Carroll (2013), who has written extensively on supervision, cited the work of Kahnman (2011) in encouraging us to be aware of unconscious (System 1) and conscious decisions (System 2).

Conscious Decisions (System 2)	Unconscious Decisions (System 1)
Deliberate	Intuitive
Explicit	Implicit
Controlled	Automatic
Analytic	Holistic
Slow	Rapid
Ad Hoc	Learned
Plastic	Patterned
Long view	Pre-packaged routines
Flexible	Procedural
Single system	Multiple system

Carroll (2013) then converted these ideas into what he termed 'brain-based supervision hints' (for supervisors), which include reviewing how System 1 and System 2 work in the practice of your supervisees. In a similar way, Van Kessel (1994 as cited in Watkins & Milne, 2014) defined the final goal of supervision as:

> *two dimensional integration' where supervisees*
> *are capable of efficiently synchronising their*

functioning with their own personal characteristic (first dimension) and of synchronising this with the properties of their professional work demands (second dimension), in a way that results in a professional self. (p. 119)

Author comment

Kaye: I would suggest to a supervisee, it is about finding out how your supervisor works in practice, whether he or she has a repertoire of alternative strategies that draw on both systems (outlined by Michael Carroll) and bring to a supervision session the capacity to teach and reflect from conscious and unconscious processes. Carroll (2013) also recommended that supervisees look for supervision that ensures that their practice remains mindful and does not become a pre-packaged routine of 'retrospective storytelling' (p. 34). He emphasised the importance of emotional literacy and that the supervisor must at times become the person to rely on when the supervisee's intuition or emotions are less than optimal with particular client(s).

When we were training as psychologists, we often had to be directly observed interviewing clients either in vivo or via recording. In our view it is equally important throughout your professional life to continue to expose your work to the scrutiny of others such as peers or a supervisor so that it is not just a process of 'case discussion'. Regularly reviewing recordings of your work with supervisors and peers is a great way to continue to grow as a therapist.

Author comment

Bruce: I will be transparent about my own supervision. I consider it very important as I have supervised the

*work of numerous graduate students in the University
of Canberra clinical program (2009–2014). I have a
fortnightly group supervision (with four senior psychologists), monthly peer supervision for an hour with a
fellow academic in clinical psychology and for 2014 I
recorded a session of my own work in Schema
Therapy that was reviewed by an overseas supervisor,
followed by an hour of individual supervision. I am sure
some colleagues might consider what amounts to
more than an hour a week of supervision excessive
but I consider it the minimum to train in Schema
Therapy and maintain my clinical work including hours
weekly of supervision. I was recently given advanced
accreditation in individual and couples therapy by the
International Society of Schema Therapy (ISST).*

There are many definitions of supervision but Crago (2013) helpfully noted:

> *a good supervisory relationship must feel 'safe' in
> much the same way as a good therapeutic rela-
> tionship and this safety is created within
> supervision in much the same ways as it is
> within therapy; by careful listening, by supervi-
> sors who place the supervisee's interests and needs
> before their own, by empathy and encouragement
> and (and when the alliance is strong enough to
> bear it) by respectful challenge of inappropriate
> or unhelpful practice. (p. 70)*

There is a balance in supervision between technique and evidence versus process and therapist self-awareness in much the same way that we look to balance the science and the art of therapy with our clients. For some people, group supervision or consultation is a more effective way to open up and to hear the struggles and methods of fellow psychologists rather than relying on the 1:1 master–apprentice mode that we equate with the term supervision in psychology.

Author comment

Kaye: If you want to get the most out of your supervision session, then think about recording sessions with clients (with their permission) and viewing these sessions with your supervisor on a regular basis. It makes the supervision real and not just about what you report to the supervisor. It also allows for deliberate practicing of micro-skills via review with your supervisor (e.g. checking whether or not the way in which you undertook cognitive re-structuring with a client was effective and how your performance could have been improved).

Counselman (2013) stated that peer consultation groups require a model of consultation that enhances a sense of safety in presenting a situation where the group members share their emotional reactions and associations rather than one person presenting a specific case issue and everyone else giving advice as resident 'experts'. She pointed out that in 'leaderless' groups, group structure including frequency and length of meetings needs to be established as well as the presentation format, whether the group is open to new members and group processes that enhance emotional and cognitive learning. Peer supervision groups or potential members can be sourced via the APS, Mental Health Professions Network or other professional associations.

CPD requirements are now part of the registration standards for ongoing registration as a psychologist in Australia. Constructing a Learning Plan has been derided by some psychologists as a 'nanny state' but it is important to have both short-, medium- and long-term learning plans that reflect private practice related skill set development.

An example of a learning plan that is orientated towards building private practice related skills might look like this:

Learning goal (short term)	Learning activity	Timeframe
Enhance capacity to deliver focussed psychological strategies as per Medicare Better Outcomes requirements	Complete CBT fundamentals course (APS online)	6–12 months

Learning goal (medium–longer term)	Learning activity	Timeframe
Further develop my skills in couples counselling	Enrol in a 12 month marital therapy training course	12–18 months
Upgrade my 4+2 qualifications to Masters level	Enrol in a Masters of Counselling Psychology	2–3 years
Learn mindfulness that I can apply to my own life and then to my work with clients	Enrol in a mindfulness class weekly for 6 months and then follow up with a mindfulness-based cognitive training (MBCT) course	12–18 months

Summary

Often we think only about the evidence base for a particular approach. But what is the evidence for the improvement of outcomes for clients via the input of supervision? Watkins & Milne (2014) in their *Handbook of clinical supervision* use research to argue that supervision should be re-named 'super listening'. There is a general consensus that clinical supervision performs the basic functions of being educative or formative, supportive or restorative and managerial or normative (p. 104). Essentially supervision is about lifelong learning and development. This is of course necessary when we live in rapidly changing professional world. Good supervision is therefore about problem clarification, reflection on what we do and decisions made with a view to developing greater self-reflection in the practitioner. It is hard to be reflective without feedback so budgeting for the time and cost of supervision is a critical part the business plan of any privately practicing psychologist.

Reflect: What was your best experience in supervision? What was your worst? How can you maximise what you have found works best for you?

Chapter 6

Ethical dilemmas:
Traps in private practice land

In this chapter we will examine some of the clinical dilemmas with ethical implications that present in private practice. Just how do we manage such complications? Consider this part of your Survival Guide 101!

Reflect: Have you had a recent ethical dilemma? Did you discuss this in supervision? Did you ring the Australian Psychological Society (APS)? Think about the process you went through.

Reviewing the ethical code (in our case, *The APS Code of Ethics* and the accompanying Ethical Guidelines) or state and federal legislation on privacy and record keeping is a start in establishing an ethical attitude. But it is not the same as understanding ethical principles and how they translate into ethical practice.

The APS Code of Ethics (2007) is based on three principles: respect for the rights and dignity of people, propriety and integrity. There are 33 accompanying guidelines on a range of topics that are continually being reviewed. The guidelines are intended to inform the practice of psychology and generally are written as a 'drilling down' exercise related to a particular area of psychology. They refer to a particular section of the broad code of ethics that is relevant to that area (e.g., working with multiple clients, working with clients at risk, or offering psychological services via the internet). The code is available to all Australian registered psychologists but the guidelines are for members' viewing only.

Brennan (2013) noted, in summarising ethical principles for practice as a mental health clinician, that our behaviour and practices in working with clients should always be informed by the core ethical principles of autonomy, beneficence, fidelity, justice, and non-maleficence. What do these principles look like in real life and how do they relate to ethical practice in a private practice setting? Let's look at some examples:

Principle	Issues that may arise in private psychological practice
Autonomy	This term refers to the client's opinions and values being respected by the psychologist. What happens in your practice when your client's goals are not the same as those you think should be the focus of psychological treatment?
Beneficence	This term refers to working in the best interest of clients. What if your client wants you to work with them on a range of health issues but their psychological treatment is supposed to be in regard to a work injury not their childhood trauma. How do you decide between the client's best interest and the policies of an insurance company paying for your services for a particular difficulty?
Fidelity	This term refers to being 'true to the client'. It could include such behaviour as being on time for appointments, being present in sessions, responding to requests for reports or copies of records in a timely manner. However, what if your client is someone who will not be dissuaded from droning on about the same issues each session or is someone about whom you have a 'sinking' feeling when you see their name on your appointment list for the day? Are you as focused and attentive to these clients as you are others?
Justice	The term refers to treating all clients equitably regardless of ethnicity, religion and so on. But what to do you do when a client expresses racist or sexist views to you or is a religious zealot? What if your client is quite wealthy but will not pay his/her session cancellation fee?
Non-maleficence	The term refers to the Hippocratic oath concept of 'do no harm'. You decide that the client with childhood trauma needs to deal with the impact of the trauma by discussing it in detail with you. In the process of doing so, your client becomes suicidal. Have you violated this ethical principle?

Other examples of ethical transgressions that can occur in private practice include:

- Operating outside of your scope of practice.

John had undertaken a two-day course in couple's therapy. He believed there was a niche market for this type of treatment in his area and advertised himself as a couple's therapist. He had a couple attend for three sessions, who stated that they had communication problems in their marriage. By the end of the three sessions, they had separated and were both attending other therapists.

- Lack of informed consent.

Melissa is a psychologist who sees individual adults. She had been treating her client Saskia, who is 18 years of age. Saskia has been self-harming and has a history of difficult relationships with her family. Her mother rang Melissa to discuss Saskia's mental health and given that Saskia's mother was paying for the sessions, Melissa took the call. Saskia's mother gave Melissa an update on Saskia's latest arguments with the family and her ongoing problems with anger and depression. Saskia found out that Melissa had discussed her treatment with her mother and left therapy.

- Inadequate record keeping.

Chris runs a busy group practice that rents out rooms to a number of other psychologists. He uses an online client booking service and also uses his tablet for clinical notes. A client file is subpoenaed and he realised that there are dates of treatment with no clinical notes and whole treatment sessions missing on the client's digital file — he meant to complete the notes at the end of the day but business demands kept getting in the way. He sent the inadequate notes to the court that had a detrimental effect on the case. His client complained about his conduct to the registration board.

- Incompetent report writing.

Susan wrote a report on her client who was facing criminal charges due to unpaid fines. In trying to help her client, Susan stated that the client had Post-Traumatic Stress Disorder although the client's problems did not meet the criteria for such a diagnosis.

When she gave evidence in court, she was cross-examined on her diagnosis and treatment of the client. Her testimony was found to be unreliable because of exaggeration. The client's case was negatively affected by her report.

- **Lack of management of counter-transference.**

John is a psychologist who experienced bullying during his school days. His practice specialised in work stress and organisational psychology. He had a contract with an agency to undertake assertiveness training with staff and came to believe that the manager was a bully due to his manner and the stories that a senior staff member told him. He decided to encourage the staff member to take these issues to the CEO and wrote a report supporting her version of events. Ultimately this lead to the sacking of the staff member as she previously applied for the manager's job and had been unsuccessful. John's contract ended with the agency.

- **Inadequate treatment of the non-improving client.**

Sarah, a middle aged woman with a long history of depressive episodes, had been attending private psychological treatment with Daniel for 12 months of weekly sessions. She continued to suffer from chronic dysthymia. Her scores on symptom measures for depression had not changed and neither had she progressed on any other outcome measures. Daniel was worried about her feeling rejected by him and decided not to raise the option of referral to another psychologist or to a psychiatrist. He felt he was offering palliative care to her to help maintain her current function. Two weeks later she attempted suicide and when asked by the CAT team why she didn't tell Daniel, she stated that she didn't want to upset him.

- **Sexual boundary violations.**

Bill was married for 25 years and his wife, who had been diagnosed with an aggressive breast cancer, had recently died. After taking a month off work, he felt he was able to return to work as a psychologist as his empty house made him feel upset and depressed. He practised by himself in a GP practice. The GP was a family friend. He had been treating a female client, Linda who had been seeking help regarding work problems. She was vivacious and seemed to like talking to him and laughed at his jokes. He ran into her at a local cafe so they sat down and had a coffee together. Next session, he talked with her about their social interaction and she stated that she liked him and would like to see him socially. Bill ceased therapy with Linda and started dating her. Six months later, their relationship finished acrimoniously and Linda complained about his behaviour to the registration board. Bill decided to close his practice and await the outcome of the complaint.

None of these examples are fictional. They are all drawn from the complaints made to registration boards. Applied ethical decision-making is an often neglected area of professional development in psychology. Unlike professions such as the legal profession, psychologists do not have a prescribed amount of ethical training to be undertaken each year.

The Ethical Decision Making Team from the APS Ethics Committee (2013) has compiled a five-step ethical problem solving process. Within that process we suggest that you put these questions to yourself:

- Would I be comfortable if my colleagues knew about this situation?

- Have I changed my usual professional practices, provided more self-disclosure than usual, avoided certain topics, ruminated after a session with a client, or felt uncomfortable or regretful?

- Are there any legal obligations that apply in this situation that are contributing to or may even override the ethical issues (e.g., a mandatory reporting obligation, a client's right of access to his/her health record)?

- Could I have prevented the issue from developing? Am I satisfied with the way I managed the situation and the processes I engaged in? Could I have done anything differently at any stage? Is there anything I can do differently in future to prevent such a situation (i.e., integrate my learning into my ongoing professional life)? (Shaw, Bancroft, Metzer, & Symonds, 2013).

Even if you are to deal effectively with most ethical dilemmas, you will need a third person to help identify 'blind spots'. The clinical encounter is inter-subjective, so often we may not be conscious of everything that is occurring with the client. It is essential to meet with a supervisor, mentor or coach to keep considering and reconsidering ethical practice with clients and in our business arrangements.

Author comment

Kaye: I have sat on tribunals where psychologists have had to answer complaints regarding their business practices, their conduct with their clients including inappropriate behaviour, poor note taking or lack of provision of reports, alleged incompetence, issues with fees, boundary violations and the like. Most psychologists who receive a notification feel panicky, affronted/angry, upset and fearful. The AHPRA Annual Report 2013–2014 notes that notifications or complaints against psychologists comprise 1.4% of the total registrant base, which is approximately 488 notifications. The AHPRA Annual Report recorded that the 65.5% of complaints against psychologists are closed after initial investigation. That said, in my experience with these cases, many of the psychologists are lacking reflective practice skills and are often disconnected from colleagues, over-worked and not attending to self-care. When their performance or conduct is found to fall short, the reaction is often to be defensive and feel aggrieved. In many cases, however, it is possible to use the experience in a positive way so as to review one's practice with a supervisor (often mandated by the

*Psychology Board of Australia in their findings and
determinations regarding the notification). I would
advise you to candidly examine your performance as a
psychologist in a number of domains which are important to safe and competent practice.*

Summary

It is essential to be reflective if you are to practice in an ethical
way. Often time is the problem, things 'done on the hop' can
be risky. Begin with asking yourself probing and pointed
questions about how you practice. Think about how you can
incorporate good supervision into your practice routine.

Chapter 7

Tricky and complex presentations in private practice

Professional psychology programs do not contain all the 'answers'. There is usually a 'trial and error' process that we later we learn what is essential for our survival as practitioners. This chapter will focus on how we maintain our psychological health while dealing with people who are at times very unwell and can be damaging to others. This is one of the key challenges of private practice since generally your clients do not come in with a warning! You may get a sense of risk after some sessions of treatment and often there is no senior practitioner, multi-disciplinary team or consulting psychiatrist that you can easily access for on-site consultation. Considering how to deal with such risky clients in advance may assist you in caring for them and yourself more effectively.

Dealing with severe personality disorders

There is a lot of 'wear and tear' in doing therapy. This is accentuated when dealing with personality disordered people. It is a multiplication of complexity and risk.

Therapy is an intimate relationship, and it is not generally with someone we have 'selected' to work with. People make appointments. They 'come through the door'. Difficult people, who have a problematic way of relating, will suddenly want our help. The following might be a wake-up realisation, 'If an individual treats his or her spouse badly, and that is pretty much a given, then why would you expect them to treat you any differently?'

Inevitably we enter the helping relationship with those we try to help and at times suffer 'friendly fire'. Sometimes a person may enter counselling with a fixed agenda, and when this fails to materialise then it is the therapist who is blamed (including making a complaint to the registration board or others such as the GP). Some people don't know how to treat anyone well. There can be a risk of violence, even potentially murder, so self-care will involve a good 'relationship alarm system'. It is foolish to deny our vulnerability.

There are 'in session' concerns. Emotional volatility can be confronting and soon well beyond our 'comfort zone' as therapists. It is easy to become too involved trying to assist a person in distress, so the danger of enmeshment is ever present. We are not immune from what Figley (1995) called 'compassion fatigue'.

Reflect: Who was the most difficult person you have treated? (Usually therapists only take a split-second to identify someone.) What made them so hard to deal with? How did they treat you as a person trying to help them?

Any patient with a personality disorder is likely to be difficult to treat. However there are additional risks with the two following categories in which the risk is especially high.

The psychopath

First, think about the Antisocial Personality Disordered with psychopathic traits. The psychopath might be reasonably easy to pick when incarcerated (think in terms of 25% of that population) but less obvious in a normal clinical setting. Their charm may initially be persuasive. It helps to know some 'give away' signs.

First think in terms of an approach to life. The life-motto of a psychopath is 'A sucker is born every minute'. Everything is said with spin. There is an ever-present coercive or manipulative element.

Bettina had a seductive way of relating to her male therapist. She wore short skirts that he found distracting. She kept trying to get him to write a 'letter of reference' so she could get a job in the accounting section of a retail outlet. But he was trying to help her with a pattern of work-related fraud. He said to her, 'Bettina I am trying to help you with a dysfunctional pattern that has been consistent in your life, while I think you are making some progress, it is not my role to 'vouch' for you'. She did not return to therapy.

Reflect: When you encounter psychopathic anger it can be highly revealing. This kind of anger is coldly instrumental and efficient — just enough is 'let out' to intimidate you into doing what they want, but no more.

Examine possible counter-transference reactions to the psychopath. Do you feel you are being 'played'? Usually this is a matter of gentle persuasion (until you resist when it can get ugly).

Robert Hare developed the Hare Psychopathy Checklist — Revised (PCL-R) Second Edition (Hare, 2003), which is the best psychological instrument for identifying this personality. Hare has also written *Without conscience: The disturbing world of the psychopaths among us* (1993), providing a good introduction to the disorder. Note that not every spouse who thinks their partner is a psychopath is correct — but some are!

There are countless self-care issues. How do we protect ourselves when treating the psychopath? The most important step is early identification. All too often a therapist will 'wake up' late and find that a line has already been crossed.

Transference, counter-transference and 'parallel processes' are often apparent in an anti-therapeutic way in providing therapy to particular personality types.

> Author comment
>> Bruce: There is a need to change our approach in treating the psychopath. Our normal therapeutic style is risky with this kind of person. We tend to lead with empathy and emotional openness, which works with pretty much everyone else, but the psychopath will be read it as being vulnerable and weak. It is an open invitation 'to be taken advantage of' in some way. Therapeutic rationalisations, like 'I should be able to help anyone', are potentially dangerous.

It is foolish to think that our clinical skills will protect us. Hare admitted that he has been taken in by the occasional psychopath and he is the world expert. Never assume you are in the clear. I have come to realise that in order to actually assist the psychopath, the essential ingredient is respect. His or her respect for you! Only in this way can you make any therapeutic progress – because you are not disregarded or held as 'beneath contempt'.

> Bernie, a forensic psychologist, visited the prison once a week to treat a number of difficult inmates. Initially Ted, who had raped a teenage girl, was contemptuous. But Bernie asked him bluntly, 'Ted what has your criminal activity ever done for you? I have a respected profession, the regard of my peers, I can leave the prison at the end of the day. I will see my wife and children tonight. What will you go back to?'. This may seem strange, even tactlessly 'rubbing Ted's nose' in what he has lost, but it may be necessary to establish that he doesn't have his 'shit together'.

There is something within us that recoils from the psychopath. You may come to appreciate some terrible aspects of their history. It can help to distinguish the person from what has been done, even when the actions are callous and hurtful to others. The person still needs the 'positive regard' that is due to everyone we treat (though with caution!).

It will not be easy to get this person into a vulnerable place where change can occur. One of the best ways is to use guided imagery where your client focuses on past hurts from others, and then makes a link to what in their current adult life feels similar. It is also important to be honest and frank. If you cannot find something to like about them, this will be sensed and the work cannot be done. It is important to confront contradictions or histories that you do not think are accurate (this might include accounts by police of a crime), perhaps as a tentative inquiry.

> Bernie said to Ted, 'I don't see how this fits, but I did read the police statements about the assault. However you have a different slant ... I am sure there are some emotional reasons why you put it out there like this ... can you help me understand these? It's hard to help you when you seem to hide yourself'.

Use your empathic confrontation skills and also the therapy relationship itself to give feedback on how their behaviours affect you.

Therapist Tip: Listen to your 'gut instincts'. If something is not quite right about someone you are treating, you might be absolutely right! Talk to your individual supervisor or raise the case in peer review. You may be advised to refer the person, which will probably be the safest option.

Borderline Personality Disorder

Treating a person with Borderline Personality Disorder (BPD) can be challenging, especially if you have not had much experience with personality trait issues and emotional dysregulation. There is no need to repeat the DSM-5 criteria, which are well known, but it is important to consider some common characteristics. A person with BPD can appear to the therapist as 'high maintenance'. And indeed, even for a skilled and experienced therapist they will feel that they will certainly fail to meet this need. There are a number of excellent training programs in working with trauma and subsequent personality difficulties and other evidence-based therapies such as Dialectical Behaviour Therapy (DBT) which are recommended for working with complex presentations.

There can be difficulties with explosive anger for some clients. It may feel like being at the foot of a volcano waiting for an eruption. But anger for a person with BPD is unlike that of the psychopath, it is unprocessed, unfocussed and can impact widely and destructively. Rage can be external with personal attacks against the therapist or anyone at hand; or internalised with self-injury or suicide attempts. The client generally lacks internal anchors for identity and emotional maturity. Relational skills may be very deficient. Moods are unstable. It can sometimes feel to the therapist during a session that they are riding a roller coaster. In some instances there can be a lack of reality testing, but this is usually stress related and somewhat transient.

> Nattie sat brooding in the session after her therapist arrived five minutes late. It was hard to shift her from her 'mood'. Nattie then accused her psychologist having another patient who was her 'favourite'. I know you spent that extra time with her — you think nothing of me.

While people with BPD tend to 'like' therapy, they can present difficulties for therapists navigating the therapeutic relationship across time. It is easy to be drawn into a kind of 'emotional psychosis', which can be confusing for the therapist and the client. You might find what Schema Therapy has labelled the Detached Protector, an emotionally numb state, even in a 'good' session, and find the patient is not available to do any productive work. There are practical difficulties with a balance of finding a therapeutic connection without reactively distancing or being fused with the client.

Warning: It can be alarming to experience counter-trans-ference of fragments of early states. You might even experience a frightening fantasy of being an infant in the care of this borderline mother or father! This can be quite disturbing. Again this might be raised in supervision or in your personal therapy.

The psychoanalytic concept of 'primitive emotional commu-nication' can be useful in understanding difficult behaviour during therapy from people with BPD. This acknowledges that some individuals will experience great distress but not be able to put that distress into words (even though that is the point of therapy). People with BPD can be poor at mentalisa-tion (Fonagy, Gergely, Jurist, & Target, 2004), so teaching them by being a good model is crucial for building a more mature approach to life. Infants who are preverbal can only cry, which distresses people, but does effectively convey the internal state of the infant. This will evoke the same internal state in the carer. It is a form of non-verbal communication, but it helps us to understand the non-conscious rationale for difficult behaviour. Infants simply have no idea how to behave better. There is no need to take it personally.

Amanda 'exploded' at Mary her therapist. She said some very unkind words and Mary was tempted to end therapy. However she took the incident to her supervisor, who discussed the concept of primitive emotional communication. Mary was able to say in the following session, 'Amanda I know you were very angry in our last session. I felt hurt by some of the things you said. I believe that you were trying to make me feel as bad as you felt at the time, so I can understand more about what you experience. Does that make sense? I just wanted to tell you that I think I get how you feel so abused.'

Reflect: Can you identify Amanda's primitive communication to Mary?

The narcissist

Wendy Behary (2013) noted:

> *self aggrandisement almost always covers up*
> *painful longings for true connection, intimacy and*
> *a sense that they're good enough ... rather than*
> *being purely entitled and spoiled, most narcissists*
> *are wounded, deprived and avoidant, burdened*
> *with unattended loneliness and shame (p. 40).*

Narcissists pick up 'fake' empathy fast so in working with them you have to be able to communicate openness with humour and keep it real — an angry challenge by the therapist when a scathing comment is made can be an unhelpful response. They are often not interested in their relationship with you or exploring it. Finding a way to help the narcissistic client to move towards self-acceptance without either inflating the self or disparaging others requires patience and working with their shame about asking for anything (McWilliams, 2011). Immediacy in the room with this type of client and confidence with your interactions with the client are prerequisites for working with this client group. Good supervision and reading about narcissism and narcissistic reactions will help you to work with these clients.

Talking about his marital problems, Dave said: 'My wife has the problem, not me. You have no idea what I have to put up with and what I do to make her and the kids happy. But it's never good enough'. When I reflected Dave's loneliness in his marriage, he switched to detached mode and told me that my 'psychobabble' ideas about relationship were of no relevance to him and that he had a perfectly fine upbringing and the only reason I wanted to talk about it was to justify the fee I was charging him.

Reflect: How do we maintain our own self-worth and self-esteem when we are the ones feeling vulnerable with narcissistic clients?

The sexual boundary

There are boundary considerations in treating disturbed people. Realistically there is some risk of crossing sexual boundaries and therapists have to be 'on guard'. Reflect on your relationship history. Have you ever had experiences dating a psychopath or borderline partner? Or at a lesser level had to deal with a partner with such traits? If you recognise this in your relationship history then you may have some unhealthy patterns of attraction.

The psychopath might be considered an example of hyper-masculine sexuality. Some may be drawn to this attribute (in spite of the danger). Additionally the borderline has hyper-feminine attributes. While this risks stereotyping, if you identify any vulnerability it is best to acknowledge and manage the risk.

Therapist Tip: It useful to develop a 10-point scale to assess your level of attraction in a given situation. Rate 9/10 as having 'run off with the person you are treating', 8/10 as losing control, and so forth down the scale. Once you have the scale, assign management strategies to each stage such as: tell my supervisor, share in peer supervision group, raise with my romantic partner, go into therapy, refer the individual (without telling them the reason!). It is useful to have a

> *two-point buffer between going beyond an acceptable*
> *boundary and a more comfortable management. And*
> *remember it is risky to play brinksmanship.*

Mary was attracted to Ben. He was charming and very good looking. She said to a colleague in her peer supervision group, 'He is like eye candy'. Ben wanted to shake hands at the end of sessions, something Mary was honest enough to admit she enjoyed. She was encouraged by her peer supervision group to rate her attraction and she said 'about 6/10'. Mary then realised this was too high to manage. Mark, one of her group, offered to see him on referral.

> *Reflect: Can you think of someone you have treated whom*
> *you found sexually attractive? How would you rate them?*
> *What management strategies did you use?*

Positive behaviours for self-care with tricky cases

Norcross & Guy (2007) wrote a useful book on self-care called *Leaving it at the office: A guide to psychotherapist self-care.* Their advice includes some of the following:

- Think about your values on a regular basis. Perhaps do a values questionnaire (from Acceptance and Commitment Therapy), or write a personal mission statement (Covey, 2004).

- Promote the positive in your life.

> *Author comment*
>> *Bruce: I discipline myself to do good things such as going to a favourite art gallery, attending a concert or finding a new restaurant. Nothing beats spending quality time with friends. Regular breaks every 3 to 6 months can become part of your annual calendar. As therapists, we deal with a lot of ugliness so we need to balance this with an emphasis on the beautiful.*

- Debrief as soon as possible after a critical therapeutic incident. Identify someone among your close colleagues whom can you ring immediately. You maybe have a mutual agreement to be available for each other as required.

- Have a peer supervision group. It is a good additional support to have individual supervision on an ongoing basis.

- Personal psychotherapy. At times this is an absolute need for any practicing therapist. In a time of stress going into therapy should be our first response not a reluctant last resort!

  Author comment
  Bruce: I have had three sessions of therapy in the last couple of years (after a significant transition). I later shared with my graduate students that I had gone to a therapist. I think this demonstrates that it is important to acknowledge 'being human' with other psychologists — including those in training such as students or supervisees.

- Healthy escapes.

  Author comment
  Bruce: I now plan two or three overseas trips a year for breaks. Also care for your physical health, including regular physical examinations: Do not forget what you tell your clients about exercise.

- Do an environmental audit of your office. How pleasant is it as a work place? Have a colleague look it over and give you feedback. One idea is to have a refresh centre with fresh fruit, drinks, or some energy food for that low point in the afternoon.

- Track your self-care, including recording what you do for a month. Sometimes it useful to have a 'decompression ritual' such as listening to music while driving from the office to home.

- Spiritual resources include meditation, mindfulness, retreats, prayer, or devotional reading Mindfulness in our own lives and spiritual renewal (via whatever methods assist you) are critical to self-care.

> *Author comment*
>
> *Bruce: I can imagine a practitioner reading this advice and thinking that my self-care strategies are a somewhat extreme. Maybe. But I am a senior practitioner with nearly 30 years of practice and I am still seeing clients. I intend to continue for at least another 10 years. The only way this will be possible is to be almost 'obsessive' about my self-care.*

> *Warning: Over the years we have treated colleagues who have gotten into trouble with registration boards and had their 'right to practice' threatened or even taken away. Almost always the problem has been one of a lack of self-care.*

Paul MacLean (1990) proposed the triune brain. This is a helpful way to think about what needs to be addressed through relaxation and self-care. Broadly, a distinction is made between the reptile, mammal and human brain (which appeared in stages according to evolutionary theory). How do reptiles relax? A man answered this with, 'Flat out on a rock in the sun.' Mammals tend to groom each other and have a lot of touch for affiliation. Humans can uniquely enjoy beauty, creativity and spirituality. The following is a slightly ridiculous image: Having a glass of wine in a spa bath, listening to a symphony by Beethoven, with your partner giving you a foot massage — activities which would cover all parts of the brain!

Conclusion

Therapy is both a challenge and a joy. Even in a day full of appointments you will find 'magic moments' that are energising. And sometimes a person will return, years later, to tell you about the difference your counselling made to them. It is a rare privilege to know you have made a lasting difference.

As psychologists we get to live a thousand lives. Of course, this is sometimes ugly and even damaging to us. But equally, we often see the courage of people who take risks and fashion a better life. We are there when much of it happens — and we can glimpse the potential of love to 'always protect, always trust, always hope, always persevere' (1 Corinthians 13:7).

Feedback Informed Treatment (FIT): How to and why you should implement it in private practice

A central point in this chapter is our fitness to practice. It is not as obvious as choosing the right tool for a job but sometimes this is what counts — the tools we rely on.

Resistance, therapeutic plateaus and getting stuck

Have you felt as a therapist as if you were 'walking on a tightrope'? That tightrope may be stretched between the points of challenging the client to achieve change and meeting them at the point where they are at. Have you seen someone for three or four sessions, but then realised that you have missed something important? This might be some assessment questions, or perhaps you did not administer a baseline measure at the outset of treatment or you should have asked for specific feedback on the effectiveness of treatment. These types of issues can emerge when we review our treatment plans with a colleague or supervisor and realise what we have missed. Sometimes we are unable to articulate goals for the therapy.

Sometimes the client will not let us know that we have 'missed the boat'. They can be very forgiving for a session or two but eventually will give up. The client has to feel they are making progress towards meeting their needs or achieving goals. When there is no perceived progress, why continue to pay for therapy?

Some concrete strategies can help. Set some measureable goals with your client. This will reduce the likelihood of passive 'yes but' statements (giving excuses as to why something you have agreed to has not happened).

It is hard for clients to change. If it was easy to change then who would need to see a psychologist? Evaluating how sessions are going for the client creates collaboration and an opportunity to evaluate progress if things are not moving forward.

Quality assurance is not clearly taught in university training courses, but it is of great importance to build a successful private practice. Bruce Wampold (2001), in *The great psychotherapy debate: Models, methods and findings*, argued that collaboration with our clients, transparency in our approach to the work and the promotion of a culture of feedback is essential. This is not just marketing or public relations, it is the results of research into what works in therapy — and what works is engagement. Wampold (2001) said that the essence of therapy is embodied in the therapist. Psychotherapy is not like medical treatment where it can be broken down into specific ingredients that are responsible for the benefit to the client. Moreover the research shows strong evidence for treatments being uniformly efficacious.

In an article by Wampold et al. (2010) regarding work in the treatment of posttraumatic stress disorder (PTSD), it was argued that trauma focused and non-trauma focused bona fide treatments work equally well in the effective treatment of PTSD. This contention was and still is controversial among those who believe that exposure therapy is the superior PTSD treatment. Of more interest, Wampold also enunciated the possible factors that are important to the successful treatment of PTSD:

Cogent psychological rationale that is acceptable to patient

Systematic set of treatment actions consistent with the rationale

Development and monitoring of a safe respectful trusting therapeutic relationship

Collaborative agreement about tasks and goals of therapy

Nurturing hope and creating a sense of self efficacy

Psychoeducation about PTSD

Opportunity to talk about trauma

Ensuring patient safety

Helping patients learn how to avoid re-victimisation

Identifying patients resources and building resilience

Teaching coping skills

Examination of behavioural chain of events

Exposure (in session and outside of session)

Making sense of traumatic event and patient's reaction to event

Patient attribution of change to his or her own efforts

Encouragement to generate and use social supports

Relapse prevention

These factors that are important to successful treatment of PTSD could be adapted to apply to many mental health presentations. They have a universality to them. Some treatments emphasise certain factors over others, or label the factors in a different way, but the key point is that there is a rich array of (common) factors in psychotherapy that improve successful outcomes for clients.

Psychotherapy is an efficacious approach for treating psychological distress and improving wellbeing that is provided in the context of a relationship between the client and the therapist. In most studies of psychological treatment conducted over the last 40 years, the average treated person is better off than 80% of the untreated sample (Minami et al.,

2008). The difficulty is that dropout rates are high (47%) and mental health professionals often fail to identify failing cases. There is a need therefore to be able to identify at an early juncture those who are not getting better and change what we are doing with them. The therapeutic relationship has been identified as the primary predictor of a positive outcome from therapy (see the International Center for Clinical Excellence[1] [ICCE], Feedback Informed Treatment (FIT) Manual series[2], published in 2012). (Bargmann & Robinson, 2012; Bertolino, Axsen, Maeschalck, Miller & Babbins-Wagner 2012; Bertolino, Bargmann & Miller, 2012;

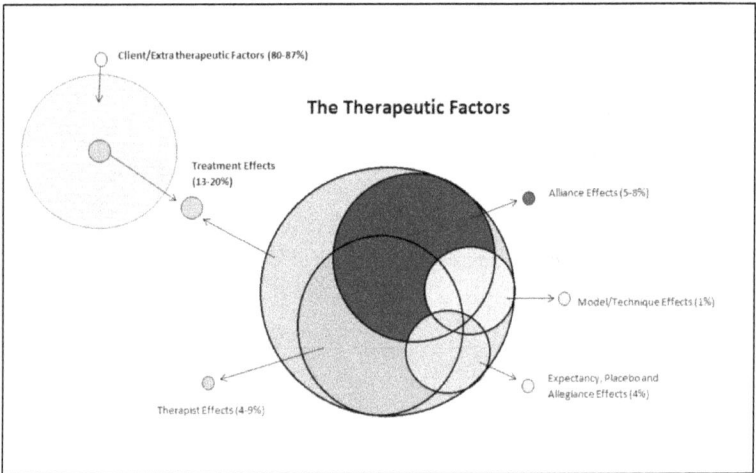

Figure 8.1 Therapeutic factors diagram.

Maeschalck, Bargmann, Miller & Bertolino, 2012; Seide & Miller, 2012; Tilsen, Maeschalck, Seidel, Robinson & Miller, 2012. The following chart illustrates the determinants of outcome from therapy.

1 https://www.centerforclinicalexcellence.com/
2 http://scottdmiller.com/wp-content/uploads/ICCE%20Core%20Competencies.pdf

The chart illustrates therapeutic factors that can be defined as follows:

- *Extra-therapeutic Factors*: Those factors that are a part of the client (such as ego strength and other homeostatic mechanisms) and part of the environment (such as fortuitous events, social support) that aid in recovery regardless of participation in therapy. They account for 80% to 87% of the variability in scores between treated and untreated clients (Wampold, 2001).

- *Treatment Effects*: These effects account for 13% to 20% of the variability in scores between treated and untreated clients (Wampold, 2001) and include:

  - Expectancy, Placebo and Allegiance (4%), which relate to both the client's and the therapist's ideas about therapy and its potential effects (e.g., positive view of treatment, faith in treatment method).

  - Model and Techniques (1%), which are those factors unique to therapy that fit with the client's preferences and expectations and provide structure to therapy.

  - Therapist Effects (4%–9%), which refers to the importance of 'who' delivers therapy that is that some therapists form more positive relationships with a broad range of clients than others.

  - Alliance Effects (5%–8%) which refers to the quality of the therapeutic relationship between therapist and client.

The evidence from outcome research illustrates that the therapeutic alliance and the therapists' capacity to form an alliance with their clients that is consistent with the client's stated goal, preferences and values and means of achieving the goal is more likely to be effective.

> *Auhtor comment*
> *Kaye: In private practice environments in particular, clients need choices and to be provided with a level of autonomy and control. Being asked to provide feedback regarding the counselling approach can assist goal attainment. Therapy is cost-effective and works largely due to general or common factors such as therapist empathy, warmth and acceptance and the therapeutic relationship or alliance.*

Miller (2012, as cited in FIT Manual 1— *What works in therapy: A primer*) summarised the research from 13 randomised controlled treatment outcome studies involving 12,374 consumers as follows:

- routine outcome monitoring and feedback as much as doubles the 'effect size' (reliable and significant change)

- decreases drop-out rates by as much as half

- decreases deterioration in the mental health of the clients by 33%

- reduces hospitalisations and shortens length of stay by 66%

- significantly reduces cost of care compared to non-feedback groups

- regular session-by-session feedback is more effective in improving outcome and reducing drop-outs (FIT Manual 1, p. 12).

The therapeutic alliance is important and this is comprised of four components: agreement on the goals, meaning and purpose of the treatment, agreement on the means and methods used, agreement on the therapist's role and accommodation of the client's preferences that is likely to consistently contribute to positive client outcomes across therapeutic approaches (Norcross, in FIT Manual 1, p. 16).

If you want to achieve expert performance in your private practice then you need to establish a baseline performance level, engage in deliberate reflective practice (that is working on skills and practice away from the counselling work itself) and obtain ongoing feedback from a coach or mentor.

These ideas can be studied online at the ICCE website (www.centerforclinicalexcellence.com) and at www.scottdmiller.com.

It is not the measures, nor is it about therapeutic acumen, but it is about the therapeutic alliance and about enhancing effectiveness with your clients. Feedback from your client is corrective. Think about how you use a GPS driving from A to B. Treatment effectiveness and feedback is enhanced by:

- regular consultation or supervision

- support within the practice you are working in or creating for the measurement of treatment effectiveness (e.g., administration staff understand why we use these methods and can explain them and intake systems and other initial information about the practice also explains the importance of this approach to the outcomes for each and every client) — creating a culture of feedback

- a data gathering system (e.g., methods of scoring and storing that data on individual clients and aggregated data from groups of clients is available to the therapist to utilise as feedback in therapy).

The two important measures to utilise are the Outcome Rating Scale (ORS) and the Session Rating Scale (SRS).

> *The ORS and the SRS are very brief feasible measures for tracking client wellbeing and the quality of the therapeutic alliance (FIT Manual 2, p. 4)*

The ORS is a brief client-rated four-item visual analogue scale measuring the client's experience of wellbeing in his or her individual, interpersonal and social functioning. The SRS is a visual analogue scale that takes less than a minute to administer, score and interpret. Items on the scale reflect the classical definition of the therapeutic alliance. The scale assesses four interacting elements, including the quality of the relational bond, as well as the degree of agreement between the client and therapist on the goals, methods and overall approach of therapy (see FIT Manual series).

The ORS is recommended to be administered at the start of each session (like taking the temperature of the client's current wellbeing) and the SRS is recommended to be administered at the end of each session (free downloads and manuals for the SRS and the ORS are available from http://scott-d-miller-ph-d.myshopify.com/collections/per-formance-metrics/products/performance-metrics-licenses-f or-the-ors-and-srs) and graphed so that if the SRS score goes down over sessions (a predictor of treatment drop-out or failure) then it allows the psychologist to discuss with the client what issues he/she wishes to work on and how this may be accomplished. The proformas for the ORS and SRS are as follows:

Outcome Rating Scale (ORS)

Name _____ Age (Yrs):____ Sex: M / F

Session # _____ Date: _____

Who is filling out this form? Please check one:

Self_____   Other_____

If other, what is your relationship to this person?

_____

> Looking back over the last week, including today, help us understand how you have been feeling by rating how well you have been doing in the following areas of your life, where marks to the left represent low levels and marks to the right indicate high levels. *If you are filling out this form for another person, please fill out according to how you think he or she is doing.*

Individually
(Personal wellbeing)

|—————————————————————————————————|

Interpersonally
(Family, close relationships)

|—————————————————————————————————|

Socially
(Work, school, friendships)

|—————————————————————————————————|

Overall
(General sense of well-being)

|—————————————————————————————————|

The Heart and Soul of Change Project

www.heartandsoulofchange.com

© 2000, Scott D. Miller and Barry L. Duncan

Session Rating Scale (SRS V.3.0)

Name _____Age (Yrs):____

ID# _____ Sex: M / F

Session # _____ Date: _____

> Please rate today's session by placing a mark on the line nearest to the
> description that best fits your experience.

Relationship

I did not feel heard, understood, and respected. |————————————————-| I felt heard, understood, and respected.

Goals and Topics

We did not work on or talk about what I wanted to work on and talk about. |————————————————-| We worked on and talked about what I wanted to work on and talk about

Approach or Method

The therapist's approach is not a good fit for me. |————————————————-| The therapist's approach is a good fit for me.

Overall

There was something missing in the session today. |————————————————-| Overall, today's session was right for me.

The Heart and Soul of Change Project

www.heartandsoulofchange.com

© 2000, Scott D. Miller and Barry L. Duncan

Author comment
> *Kaye: When I raise this suggestion with supervisees they often have questions about using the SRS and the ORS.*

There is a degree if uncertainty on how to best use these scales:

- The psychologist administers the ORS and the SRS intermittently citing time pressures and does not graph the results, nor show them to the client nor bring them to supervision (this could be termed as being enthused by the idea/philosophy of FIT but being uncertain about how to include the measures and feedback in working with their clients).

- The psychologist administers the ORS regularly but does not administer the SRS often citing that clients object to it and always score him/her '40' (this could be termed the 'no news is good news' scenario).

- The psychologist states that the ORS and SRS do not fit with their therapeutic modality of choice (e.g., CBT, ACT, Emotion-focused therapy). They prefer to measure the symptoms of the client regularly using screening tools such as the Depression Anxiety and Stress Scale (DASS) to demonstrate efficacy to themselves or to a third party payer such as a workers compensation scheme. The fact that the measure may not alter or that they are not sure what changes in the responses of the client means to the therapy content or process is often inexplicable to the practitioner.

Reflect: How do you know that you are doing a good job with a client? It is easy to think we are making progress, but what is the measure? Discuss this in supervision and welcome new ideas. Consider downloading the FIT manuals or undertaking online training in FIT. Think about subscribing to one of the data gathering sites (www.fitoutcomes.com or www.myoutcomes.com for example) and utilising data gathering via digital administration of the measures on a tablet/iPad device along with other psychometric self-report tests via various apps mentioned in Chapter 4. Consider FIT principles and practices as a way of defining your practice approach versus other practices around you. Use the feedback platform as an overall philosophy for your practice (e.g., feedback to referrers, feedback to clients). Consider undertaking webinar training sessions in the approach.

Learn from the 'super shrinks'

When setting up a practice, you can learn from both the mistakes of others and from the top performers. Miller, Hubble & Duncan (2007) writing about the development of a culture of feedback in psychotherapy, noted three lessons we can learn from the 'super shrinks':

- *Lesson 1: Step outside your comfort zone.* Push the limits of the effectiveness of your performance. This means identifying clients who aren't responding to your usual therapeutic approach and addressing the lack of progress in a positive, proactive way that keeps them engaged while you collaboratively seek new directions for the treatment.

- *Lesson 2: Determine client repsonse.* As clearly as possible determine how clients are responding to treatment and their degree of improvement. Assess these known predictors systematically with reliable, valid instruments. The authors suggest the ORS and the SRS.

- *Lesson 3: Seek, obtain, and maintain the highest possible level of consumer engagement.* Clients usually drop out of therapy for two reasons: the therapy is not helping (thus, the need to monitor outcome); or the alliance, the fit between the therapist and client, is problematic. Clients who do not feel they're making progress, or feel turned off by their therapist, will leave. Accordingly, the most direct way to improve effectiveness is keep people engaged in therapy.

To Do:

Discuss with colleagues the above points that distinguish effective therapists. If you have a peer supervision group this would be a good place to begin the discussion and your reflection about how you practice.

> *Author comment*
>
> *Kaye: I have been using these measures since 2001. I have had my ups and downs in terms of consistently administering them with all clients. I have had various responses such as becoming 'too busy' to do them, 'too grandiose' about my own performance (i.e., believing I don't need this feedback method but can intuit or ask the client for feedback and this will suffice) and just stopped being as reflective in my own practice as I would like to be. Supervising other psychologists who are using these measures has made me think about the measures as a way of ensuring competence and growth for practitioners as well as impacting positively on the effective treatment for clients. I believe that using these measures in your private practice will be a very important investment and one which will pay back in many ways over your career.*

Chapter 9

Record keeping, case notes and writing reports

Maintaining clinical records is an absolute requirement for clinical practice. Potentially this is an area we can get into difficulties with the registration board. Generally we get only vague suggestions of what constitutes a good clinical record (King, 2010).

What should be included?

What is usually specified for records includes the client's demographics, referral data, significant aspects of therapy sessions, psychometric test results, case planning, and supervision and discharge records.

The legal requirement in Australia, including for psychologists, is outlined in the *Privacy Act 1988* (Cth). This Commonwealth legislation informs more local state or territory legislation, overriding those if there is any conflict between those pieces of legislation (Office of the Australian Information Commissioner, 2012). The Privacy Act has a set of principles that outline the conditions under which information is collected, utilised, managed and accessed. It also protects the rights of patients to access all aspects of their clinical record with some limited exceptions. The Act also requires that records contain information that is relevant to the provision of services, and should be 'accurate, complete and up to date' (*Privacy Act*, 1988, p. 212).

In a legal context the clinical record becomes the evidence of fact about what has occurred in psychological treatment (Harris et al., 2009). In investigating complaints, health registration boards have previously utilised clinical records as a means of establishing whether a treating professional is competent in diagnosis, treatment planning and delivery. In this way clinical records provide an avenue for review not only for patients who have concerns about services received, but also for psychologists who may be required to justify their practices. While privacy is clearly valued, in Australia a practitioner's records are not given privacy when clinical records are called into evidence. This can create considerable anxiety for both psychologists and patients when clinical records are examined in legal settings (Jenkins, 2003).

> Reflect: Think for a moment about how you keep your records. Has this changed over the years? Have there been any changes since you began?

> Think: If a colleague were to take over the treatment of your client, would he or she have a clear idea of your therapy from your notes?

Professional guidelines

The Australian Psychological Society (APS) has established a code of conduct. Through this document, and other publications for their members, the APS informs psychologists of the professional standards for practice. Generally the information outlined for psychologists follows what is specified in legislation. It is important to distinguish fact from opinion, but how this is done is not especially clear. In 2010, the APS specified that information should only be what is relevant to treatment. This included date, time and place of treatment, who was present, the nature of services, and any actions taken. This brief list was criticised as not guiding psychologists in relation to what specifically is and is not necessary to document (King, 2010).

There is a range of practitioner views about what should be included. Sometimes this information is determined by a treatment perspective; for example, some have advocated that a practitioner record reflections about transference and counter-transference (Plessis & Hirst, 2006). It is also unclear how to maintain confidentiality with couple, family or group sessions.

Many authors argue that clinical records should primarily be utilised by psychologists to ensure that patients are receiving appropriate care (Harris et al., 2009; Thomas, 2010). We agree with Thomas that recommendations from supervision should be included in the record, as this can document the efforts of the psychologist to critically evaluate his or her practice and to address any risk issues.

There has been almost no research about what psychologists put in their notes. A study by Ladd (1967) is outdated and of little relevance to contemporary practice in Australia.

> *Author comment*
>
> *Bruce: One of my students, Lisa Bradford, carried out research that was published (Bradford & Stevens, 2013). In this study 18 registered psychologists were interviewed and asked to briefly audit a file of a patient that they had recently worked with. The psychologists were asked to confirm the presence or absence of possible file contents from a clinical record checklist. The purpose of the study was to establish*

whether psychologists are aware of the legislation that underpins clinical regards and their compliance with respect to this legislation. This included the format of clinical notes, the amount and types of information documented and the typical contents of clinical records. The findings of the study were that there is a high degree of variability as to how psychologists keep and maintain records and that time pressure was often a factor in poor record keeping. The study suggested that clinical records need to be both a historical account of what occurred in therapy as well as a means of generating hypotheses, case formulation and progress towards agreed goals.

What to include

To state the obvious, a psychologist cannot write down every word said in a session. It is possible to audio record and even video every session but this would provide additional problems without much benefit. So we must be selective. It is necessary to clearly demonstrate that an assessment was done. This must include risk assessment if relevant to the case. A genogram is very helpful in assessment to gather a history of mental illness and relationship instability in the family. It also provides a systemic family perspective. There should be some evidence that you inquired about the individual's history of say depressive episodes, psychotic vulnerability, and previous psychological or psychiatric treatment. It is often helpful to have a brief psychometric test such as the Depression Anxiety Stress Scales 21 (DASS-21). If issues are more complex a multiscale such as the Personality Assessment Inventory (PAI) can be very helpful (any profiles produced should be included in case notes). It is not necessary to try to be exhaustive or interrogate our patients in the first session when it vital to establish an empathic connection and begin the working alliance.

In subsequent sessions it is practical to have an aide-memoire to help you recall what was said. Working notes may also be of assistance.

> *Author comment*
>> *Bruce: But this should not be extensive or even the main focus, though I recall beginning my therapeutic career thinking this was the point of notes. We need to see that notes are primarily a record of treatment, so another clinician can take over the case with some understanding of the need for treatment, your approach and whether there was a response. It also provides a method of accountability.*

Key learning points

Files should contain:

- GP referral and mental health treatment plan (MHTP; if Medicare funded case)
- a genogram
- a pro-forma clinical assessment which could include the presenting problem, your formulation of the situation, and pertinent history
- a confidentiality agreement or consent form
- psychometric tests used
- evidence of a treatment plan and interventions used (focussed psychological strategies and/or psychological therapies in case of Medicare audit)
- contemporaneous notes that record treatment.

Need to record

> Reflect: If there is a complaint or court case regarding your
> client, your notes will probably be subpoenaed. Do you think
> you will get the 'benefit of the doubt' if something that
> needed to be done was not recorded in your notes (espe-
> cially if your client testifies that it was not done)? It is not
> wise to take such a chance.

The implication of this is that we must record the essentials of treatment.

Brett saw Mary after an unexpected separation. She had a brief reactive depression, from which she fully recovered after six sessions of treatment. Brett made a diagnosis of Major Depressive Disorder single episode with mild symptoms (from DSM-5). He did a genogram and took a brief history. Brett did not consider Mary was at risk of suicide and this was noted with her response, 'No, I would never do that to my children!' He recorded that his evidence-based treatment was Cognitive Behaviour Therapy (CBT). He included some record of his interventions including psycho-education about negative thoughts, he encouraged a thought diary and behaviour activation. Mary's response to treatment was noted. He re-tested her with the DASS 21 and noted that her depression score had improved with treatment. He recorded his understanding of their final session and how she might return to therapy if needed in the future. His file included: Confidentiality Agreement, two DASS profiles, a letter from her GP and MHTP.

This would probably be similar to the notes of most psychologists. If Brett discussed Mary in supervision it should have been acknowledged. It would be even better to include a CBT Case Formulation. At best our clinical notes are places to generate and document hypotheses that are relevant to our formulation of the case (Bradford & Stevens, 2013).

To Do:

Think about what takes most of the space in your notes. If it is what is said, to help you remember the flow of sessions, then I would recommend a greater emphasis on assessment and treatment. If you ever have to defend your treatment of a patient, you will be grateful of the care you have taken. It is not a question of how extensive, but how focused.

> *Bruce: I tend to write my notes in session, saving time and making sure it is done, so I must be very economical in what I write. Think about having a checklist at the front of your files that shows that you have covered all the necessary documentation for that client.*

> *Reflect: How often do you look over your notes? What is the purpose of this? What do you tend to note? How do your records fulfil what you want from them in practical terms? Notes should be helpful to review prior to the next session with a client and should provide a guide to planning for sessions. The mix of client statements and your notes of treatment plans and outcomes depend on the client's presentation. It can be useful to review notes particularly with longer term clients. Use different coloured highlighters to show repeated themes, particular aspects of the client's narrative, relevant life events reported to you and then use these highlighted notes to review your current progress with the client.*

Opinion versus fact

It is not well known that this is a requirement of legislation. In the study none of the practitioners knew it was necessary (Bradford & Stevens, 2013).

Author comment
> Bruce: I would keep this clear in a written report, but
> just how do we do this in our notes? I would recom-
> mend that opinion should be included under a
> heading like 'Case Formulation' (Berman, 2014).
> Another possibility is with diagnosis, say 'Rule out
> Borderline' or note a differential diagnosis. Or simply
> add a '?' to a sentence of opinion. Some psychologists
> hold the view that the fewer notes you take the better,
> and believe that it is a way of avoiding trouble;
> however, the reality is actually the opposite — the less
> your write, the more vulnerable you are legally and
> professionally to misconduct accusations.

Every practitioner experiences time pressure. It is easier to take contemporaneous notes and to start out in your career doing so — it is a practice that will be useful and efficient. If you do record later, say directly into a computer, I would only do this from my session notes that are also kept as a record. There is no distinction in Australia between the clinical record and working notes which may be considered disposable (King, 2010). Don't throw anything away! This is really diffi-cult if you use rough notes and then insert text into an electronic file.

Supervision notes are also potentially part of a file and form part of the working notes regarding that file.

Author comment
> Kaye: I have found it helpful to insert supervision notes
> into files written on a different coloured piece of paper
> that allows me to easily locate the supervision discus-
> sion and outcome when planning further sessions. If
> there is an opinion that the supervisor offers regarding
> your client and the treatment of that person, then it

can be noted that it was the opinion of the supervisor on the supervision notes.

Writing reports

Writing reports is an essential aspect of any psychology practice. It is helpful to understand the difference between a treatment report and an expert report. Consider the audience the report is prepared for. The first question you should ask yourself is 'Who is the report for?' and 'Is it a reasonable request?' If, for example, you have conducted two sessions of treatment and there is a request for a report to use in the Family Court, it is likely to be premature. Realistically you can say nothing other than you have just begun therapy. With areas such as Workers Compensation the insurer or agency might require periodic reports to pay for treatment.

The process of writing a report to another professional requires a different approach. A mental health professional, a psychiatrist, a GP, psychologist, and so on. will have an understanding of the language we use, whereas it is possible that a lawyer might misunderstand what we are trying to say. When writing to lawyers, use simple jargon-free language. When writing the treatment report, it is important that you maintain boundaries around what exactly treatment is. Areas such as the person's presentation, the reported history, their diagnosis, and the type of treatment undertaken are all within the realm of a treatment report. However, even if someone has conducted a comprehensive assessment, offering a risk assessment based on treatment becomes a very questionable area. Providing a comprehensive assessment based on treatment is, likewise, difficult.

When you are writing a legal report try to understand the role of the judge. He or she is required to make certain findings. Those findings in criminal law might be guilty or not guilty, and then what the sentence should be. In family law the decision would be where the children are to live, whether to allow a relocation, and how much time the children should spend with the other parent. This aspect of the judicial role is called the ultimate issue. In writing a report, it is important to understand that the expert witness provides all the information to the judge to help them with the next logical step, that is, to address the ultimate issue. Psychologists who make those findings in their report run the risk of having a difficult time in court. The judge might not appreciate 'trespassers on their territory'!

Author comment

> Phil: My advice to a psychologist starting out in private practice is to ensure that you attend good professional development workshops about how to write reports for Court. It is likely that your training has equipped you with information on how to write to other medical professionals, but little for legal professionals.

While writing legal reports is quite a lucrative activity, it is important that you practice within your area of competency. Therefore, before seeking a role as a forensic assessor it is critical to ensure that you have the necessary competence to conduct the types of assessments you have been requested to do.

It is wise to be very careful about the distribution of reports. Only provide reports to the person who has requested it. The danger with legal reports is if other people access the report it may create legal complications, such as breach of privilege.

When a report is completed, especially in the legal arena, it is possible for the lawyers to provide what is called an errors and omission review. If they read the report and find that you have made an error, or have missed out something of any note, it is perfectly acceptable to make those changes. Do not feel that this is pressure to change your opinion.

In regard to costing the report, you will need to find out how much people normally charge within the profession for the type of report you are providing. Lawyers charge for everything from photocopying to phone calls. Consequently, psychologists writing legal reports are entitled to payment. It is important to find out beforehand exactly who is going to pay you, and how much.

> *Author comment*
>
> Bruce: *It is very important to have money in trust or an assurance from the lawyer that you will be paid. I have had parts of reports not paid for in family law when a number of parties agree to the report but then a person, usually unhappy with the report, refuses to pay. With criminal law do not trust the accused to pay. You can ask for the cost of the report in advance.*

Final warning

In the confidential world of a psychology office, we take notes either during or immediately after the session with our client. If there is a reason why that client is involved in some sort of legal situation, whether it is in the Family Court, relating to criminal proceedings or some other jurisdiction, and if the court believes those notes from the therapy session may be of relevance to the issue they are asked to look at, then the court is allowed to access that information. This is generally via subpoena, but may occur pursuant to a different process.

It is important to understand that once subpoenaed, it is very hard to refuse to produce the material. There is helpful information and some good books that discuss subpoenas; for example, *Surviving the witness box: Expert opinion in court*

(Watts, 2009). The essential point is that any material generated in your office needs to be seen as a potential legal document. Your therapy notes may need to be produced in court. Do you consider this when you write a letter to a GP? This is a confidential letter between yourself and the GP about the client. But if the GP's file is subpoenaed then that confidential letter is now in the court, being read by all of the parties.

> *Author comment*
> *Bruce: I was recently required to produce a copy of my notes pursuant to a search warrant. I was involved in treating someone later involved in a murder inquiry. There is even 'less room to move' under those circumstances, so I fully complied with the police in that matter.*

The best way to avoid legal difficulties is to keep good and accurate records, be prudent in your practice, ensure that you have Professional Indemnity Insurance, and work within your areas of competence. If somebody raises legal issues in relation to you, it is important to seek both professional and legal advice as soon as possible.

In setting up a practice it is important that you have policies in relation to Freedom of Information and National Privacy Principles, release of information, as well as storage of information. There are various guidelines, particularly through the APS, which can assist you in developing these aspects.

As a society we understand that information about individuals needs to be made available to individuals. Consequently, Freedom of Information Acts and National Privacy Principles allow for the disclosure of information about individuals that you have on file. While there are limits to confidentiality, it is critical that you understand the need for privacy principles, and that you put in place in your practice the necessary structures to cover for the appropriate release of information.

In relation to anything you record, not only is it potentially accessible by the court, but your client can also read it. Therefore, write your material in a way that is sufficiently comprehensive but straightforward enough to minimise misunderstanding.

Individuals need to be accountable for their behaviour. If somebody commits an act, or fails to take an action, which results in the accidental harm of someone, and that incident could have been avoidable, then the person is to be held accountable. This is called the law of negligence. If you deliberately hurt someone, you can be considered to have committed a criminal act, but if you fail to take an action which a reasonably prudent psychologist would have taken, then you may be potentially liable to be sued if that action caused harm.

You may be subpoenaed for notes that you feel are inadequate. You may feel embarrassed, but never add to your notes of a session after the fact. You may feel tempted, but it has happened and worked out badly for some practitioners. You can add to your notes, but include the date on which you wrote a further reflection (e.g., after having supervision on the case).

To Do:

Think about where you have confidential information. Make sure your files are stored securely while the file is active and also for seven years post-treatment (adults). For further advice make contact with your professional association regarding particular requirements.

Question of release of information

This is a complex question. Our legal context is constantly changing, so we are reluctant to try to address this in any detail.

We recommend that you talk to the APS professional advisor regarding the issues of any particular case.

> *Author comment*
> *Bruce: I find that insurance companies and compensation schemes are now asking for client records. The request will come with a signed authorisation.*
> *However it is not clear to me that our client was fully aware of what was signed, nor would he or she keep that in mind speaking to us in session. I have a rule of not providing notes unless subpoenaed.*

To Do:

Discuss in supervision your practice of note taking. Write down this information in your record of supervision.

Note: Files are to be kept for seven years, or longer if it involves notes about a child client.

Chapter 10

Cross-examination: Preparing for court and giving evidence

It is simply a fact — a psychologist who treats patients cannot avoid court. Many try, but in time most practitioners will need to give some kind of evidence in court.

You might consider yourself 'court phobic', but this is a completely 'curable condition'. What we will try to convey in this chapter is how easy it is to prepare for court and to become familiar with some of the common pitfalls. In reading this chapter, you will take a huge step toward dealing with any reluctance to give evidence (and to manage your anxiety).

When psychologists look foolish in court

Maybe you have heard a psychologist relate a humiliating experience about going to court. Such 'campfire horror stories' get around and sometimes become more colourful with time. When we see psychologists having difficulty in court, it is usually because of a foolish mistake that even a 'Psychology 101' student should not have made.

> *Author comment*
> Bruce: I was in the Family Court offering evidence about a father's use of a child's nickname. A child psychologist wrote a report, quoted a source but did not

> check the primary source. The barrister looked up the
> original article and the clear meaning was different to
> that conveyed in the report. The psychologist looked
> foolish under cross-examination, but presumably no
> more than if a university lecturer had challenged an
> essay with a similar mistake.

It is possible to look foolish by not understanding the legal process and overstepping your role in offering an expert opinion. Consider the following levels of observation or opinion:

- observing behaviour: 'He was wringing his hands'
- perception of mental state: 'He appeared anxious'
- formulation: 'The anxiety during the interview was consistent with a general observation of trying to please others'
- diagnosis: 'It was consistent with Generalised Anxiety Disorder'
- relationship to a legally relevant question: 'At the time of the offence, his anxiety was so overwhelming that he failed to consider the consequences of his behaviour'
- elements of the ultimate issue: 'Although he was anxious at the time of the offence, he was able to reflect on the consequences of his behaviour, he knew the nature and consequences of his acts'
- ultimate legal issue: 'He was sane at the time of the offence'.

Try to avoid trespassing on legal territory (both elements and the ultimate issue). It is also wise to be modest in your opinion. For example:

Mark, a forensic psychologist, carried out an injury assessment. He gave a malingering test, which the person failed. In Mark's conclusion he said that he failed a specific test, and expressed some doubts about the person's presentation but did not conclude, 'He was found to be malingering'.

If you have any doubts about a diagnosis, it is best to be cautious. A diagnosis of Adjustment Disorder is easier to defend than Post-Traumatic Stress Disorder if there is any uncertainty.

Sometimes a judge may ask for your opinion and recommendations (especially in family law). If you are asked a direct question by the judge while giving oral evidence, then simply give an opinion as requested. You might qualify what you say with something like, 'I can only express an opinion on psychological grounds, but I would recommend that the relocation not be allowed (an ultimate issue in a family law case).' Then state your reasons.

Warning: It is risky to use legally defined concepts in expressing an expert opinion. We can too easily presume that we know more than we do. The law is not our area of expertise. For example do not use 'nervous shock' (commonly used by lawyers), but make a diagnosis of Post-Traumatic Stress Disorder (DSM-5 criteria) if appropriate.

How will you end up in court?

Phil Watts wrote *A reliable witness* (2004, updated 2009), which outlined various pathways to court. The most common is because you have treated a patient, had your notes subpoenaed, or wrote a treatment report. If you do a lot of forensic work then you will commonly be called into court. Watts distinguished:

• court appointed expert

• agreed expert

- party expert
- paper expert
- second opinion expert.

This list is in decreasing order of how the court will perceive the objectivity or strength of your evidence.

Remember that for most psychologists their first experience of court will probably be as a result of writing a treatment report. In this case our expertise simply rests on having seen the client in counselling, so our role as an expert is generally limited to the treatment provided. Always include in the introduction in your treatment report template something like the following statement:

> *Please note: This is an initial assessment and treatment report that is limited in scope. If this matter is to proceed legally then I would recommend an independent assessment to be completed by a clinical or forensic psychologist or psychiatrist to more fully advise the court.*

If we are cautious then it is much 'harder' to get into trouble.

It is important to be cautious about what we write in a report — any report that we sign makes us accountable as psychologists. Do not express any opinion for which you do not have clinical evidence.

Vince was treating Mary. He had heard in many sessions how her husband had a violent temper. When the couple separated, Mary asked him to write a report that supported her in her application to have their children reside only with her. Vince was tempted to express the opinion that her husband was totally unsuitable to parent the children. Fortunately he saw his supervisor who warned him not to express any opinion about a person 'sight unseen'.

Remember: If your report is clear and objective it will reduce the possibility of having to give evidence.

Know your role

Author comment

> Bruce: Few of us come to court feeling as expert as we would like to. In 1994, all I had going for me was a degree in psychology and having my court phobia mostly under control. But after a year or so I gained experience and gradually grew in confidence. This was achieved through becoming more active in offering expert opinion on a range of topics. If I was to be paid for writing legal reports, then I had to be prepared to have that opinion tested by cross-examination. Gradually I came to appreciate that the expectation of the court will vary, from a treatment report to a party report and up the chain when much more is expected if we are appointed by the court. In my experience we are unlikely to be called in with an injury report (1% of the time, most settle before court), criminal (maybe 10% of the time), and family or child protection issues (maybe 30%). So family law is the easiest area in which to gain court experience!

You might think of your expertise in terms of:

- Core strengths (i.e., where you might have clinical experience and a good idea of recent research).

- What is psychological but maybe outside your ability to offer expert opinion?

- The in between. This is a grey area where we have some experience and understanding, so this gives some basis for an opinion, but perhaps one expressed with caution. The onus is on us to do extra research, ask peers, or get supervision if we write a report. It can be an area in which we are growing in expertise and important to our development.

Author comment

Bruce: I will not offer any opinion on medical questions such as drug effects and there are areas of psychology beyond my expertise including brain injury. We have limits. Generally, when we are being cross-examined there is no expectation that we know everything. If asked in court about something outside your expertise: Simply admit your ignorance and never try to bluff.

To do:

Put as much preparation as possible into the report given to the solicitor. If it is shoddy then it is impossible to defend. If it is clear in reasoning, justified in conclusions and based soundly on empirical testing then you will be grateful that you spent the extra time when you are sitting in the witness box.

Reflect: What is your core area of strength? Can you see yourself offering an opinion to the courts in this area? If so then you are not far from being ready to offer expert opinion.

Even if you are providing a treatment report, try to make it look as professional as possible. Start with the model of a forensic expert report. Keep to plain English and avoid psychobabble! Psychological terms should be explained. It is safest to describe behaviour rather than use an overall term such as Domestic Violence. It is best to avoid any emotive language and be matter of fact in tone (or the report can be challenged because you took a dislike to a party). Criteria for diagnoses from DSM-5 can be given in appendices. Openly declare any limits in data gathering; for example, 'I did not interview the father in this matter ...' — then state the implications of your opinion. Remember that your report can set off a legal process and determines how you will be treated in court, for example which side will perceive you as hostile to their case!

> *Author comment*
>
>> *Kaye: Practitioner reports are often requested in worker's compensation or motor vehicle accident compensation cases. If you are writing a treatment report do not be tempted to become their advocate nor to develop an extensive criticism of the compensation scheme case management system in the report. Stick to your role and your opinions as the treating psychologist but don't become the judge, jury and executioner!*
>>
>> *Bruce: In writing court reports it is best not to use he or she 'reported that' or 'stated that' in every sentence. It becomes laboured and I would prefer to use it to express some doubt, 'Mr Smith had a blood alcohol reading (.08) but he reported to me that he never drinks more than four standard drinks on social occasions'.*

Research: preparing for court

You are expected to take a copy of your report to the court and all notes including raw data for testing. It is best to take good notes, for example I will use quotation marks and include exactly what the person has said in the report. Quotes are common in my reports, since it adds vividness, and my notes can always back this up. A number of years may have passed since you last saw the person — especially in an injury case. I have to read my notes before going to court since I rarely remember everything about the particular case.

Sometimes a case is complex and may include a thick file of affidavits, previous reports and other legal material. It may be useful to colour tab important sections of the file so you can find it quickly while under cross-examination. It is not necessary to bring all the affidavits to court (these can be provided), but it is required that you list in your report what you have read.

> *Tip: Have copies of the Expert Code of Conduct for the various courts and be familiar with the principles before you give evidence. Note whether there is an expectation that you have viewed subpoenaed material from other sources such as reports from Child Protection Agencies.*

As psychologists we routinely come across a lot of research. However, in the witness box it may be difficult to recall details of findings.

> *Author comment*
> *Bruce: I remember being cross-examined about profiles of paedophiles. I was on the spot and really grilled by a good barrister. I had a mental blank and while I could recall some relevant information, I knew that my performance had been poor. After my embarrassment wore off, I realised that I had heard a keynote address at the APS National Forensic Conference two months before on exactly that issue! I then created a system to summarise and index research that I could bring to court. I have found it useful to cite relevant research in giving evidence.*

Accessing research articles on the issues relevant to the court case that you will be asked to comment on is good practice and can assist the veracity of your opinion. Make sure that you familiarise yourself with the research. Have a photocopy of the pages from the manual on reliability and validity for any psychological test you have used (it is rare that you will be asked about this, but helpful to have on hand). It is also useful to bring a copy of DSM-5.

What is most helpful to the court is when research results are counter-intuitive (for example with sexual abuse indicators, noting that child victims of violence but not sexual abuse often act out sexually). Another example of a surprising research finding was that of Rind, Tromovitch, and Bauserman (1998). The authors found that 72% of females reacted negatively at the time, only 33% of males with 42% looking back on the experience as positive. This is counter-intuitive since we expect sexual abuse to have catastrophic consequences.

> Author comment
>> Bruce: Over the years I have noticed that experts like Dr Ken Bryne or Dr Brent Waters, who are well known in legal circles, are able to cite relevant research and frankly it has amazed me how they do it so well. Now I have an index system and a book to take to court, I can perform better and it naturally helps to add to my professional reputation.

Always take a CV into court. Just add some copies of it to your book or folder. It is also a good idea to bring the subpoena since it will have the address of the court where you are to appear. It is easy to make a mistake and embarrassing if you cannot find the court.

> Tip: Talk to the lawyer who has asked you to appear in court
> or for whom you wrote the report. While this rarely happens,
> even a brief word can help you to appreciate the issues
> being considered.

If you really are petrified about giving evidence for the first time, then I recommend taking a beta-blocker (which is commonly used by singers and musicians before performing). This blocks the adrenaline rush and will keep your voice steady (if that is a concern to you).

Most psychologists seem to have the idea that cross-examination is like being an undergraduate and facing an oral exam by the Professor of Psychology. The reality is that you know far more about psychology than almost any barrister, which is why you are the expert!

In the witness box

Court really is something of a game — a very serious game, but still a game. The legal participants rarely take it personally, no matter how badly they seem to act towards 'my learned friend' at the bar table. Sometimes what happens seems familiar but is different. As Phil Watts said, 'Things which make common sense and are obvious are overlooked while, at other times, procedures become bogged down with strange rules and apparently petty details' (2004, p. 1). When this happens I just sit back and wait for the skirmish to finish, and then questions to me will continue. Often I will have no idea what was resolved. However the law is mostly about a just procedure, so the rules of evidence are important to the process and hopefully protects the rights of all who are involved.

The first thing is that we are sworn in, taking either an affirmation or an oath on the Bible. The expert witness has the role of assisting the 'fact finder' (judge or jury) by presenting scientific, technical or specialised knowledge. This is why our credentials are important. Mostly, questions are limited to your name, professional address and highest degree.

> Author comment
>
> Bruce: I will tend to offer my academic appointments (Professor at Charles Sturt University, clinical and forensic psychologist, etc.). This stage is called the voir dire but generally it is a formality, especially if you are well known to the court. At this point you might be asked for a copy of your CV (though you should attach a brief CV to all reports or even brief expressions of opinion). You might feel that your qualifications are 'a bit thin' if you are a recent graduate and have limited experience. Do not bluff, simply state your areas of academic training and experience (however limited). It is up to the court to accord your evidence the weight it deserves. It is all part of gaining experience.

There are two main approaches that can be adopted by courts: the adversarial method, which is commonly seen in criminal and civil courts and the inquiry method, which is commonly seen in tribunals. The Family Court was set up as inquisitorial but has a strong adversarial aspect. What is most relevant to you in court is that with the inquiry method the judge is more likely to ask you direct questions.

> Author comment
>
> Bruce: I think it is helpful to address the barrister by name. As I write this, I am just back from court where the two barristers were Mr White and Mr Livingston. I spoke to both by name. This allows more of a 'level playing field' in that we address each other as equals. This is slightly disconcerting to the barristers who expect to be able to intimidate even experts 'on their ground'.

In this it is important to look like an expert, so conservative professional clothes are an asset. Watch the other extreme — excessively expensive watches or jewellery can give the impression to a jury that your testimony has been bought! Keep your testimony clear and jargon free. Charlene Steen advised:

> Jurors are extremely sensitive to how the expert
> witness presents him/herself, and will be offended
> if the expert appears biased, dishonest, argumen-
> tative, or pompous.

If possible display confidence but not arrogance. Be careful to explain any 'psychobabble', that is any terms not widely understood by the general public.

Sometimes you will be brought into court as a witness of fact and not as an expert witness. The role of a witness of fact is simply to state what treatment was given, 'Mr Smith was seen four times in individual therapy and then referred to a pain management program.' If your role is not clear then ask the judge in court.

> Author comment
>
> Bruce: I find that it is helpful to face the barrister when
> he or she is asking the question, but then face the judge
> (or rarely the jury) when giving a reply. There are various
> views on this, including some experts who will only face
> the judge, but I find this rigid and unnatural.

There is a difference between direct and cross-examination. The first barrister to address you is generally the 'friendly' side and will give you more latitude to express your views, including why you reached a conclusion. This is called *Examination-in-Chief.* The other barrister will *cross-examine*, but in my experience rarely restricts your answers. You might be asked about sources of information, assumptions on which opinions have been based, degree of certainty of an opinion, validity and deficits of all sources, if testing instruments were administered personally and correctly, and why the opinions of opposing experts might be different. Both barristers may later have an opportunity to redirect questions but the scope is limited to topics already raised. There may also be additional barristers; for example, if there are two or more defendants in a criminal trial or a child representative in the Family Court. Sometimes the judge will ask clarifying questions.

Professor Don Thompson, barrister and psychologist, at an APS National Conference, emphasised that is important to listen carefully to the question and respond to it. He recommends a 'just right' balance of not saying too much or too little. Saying too much opens you up to hostile questions. Focus on the question, answer precisely and say if you don't know the answer. If you need to give ground on a point, simply do it. This is always preferable to trying to stick to a lost point (David Childs barrister, cited by Watts, 2004, p. 116).

If you want to build up a forensic practice, how you perform under cross-examination is very important. Think, for a moment, about the lawyer's concerns in a legal matter. The matter is in court and he or she has a favourable report from an expert (Stevens, 2008). But rather than being able to base the case upon this evidence, the expert crumbles under cross-examination and the evidence becomes worthless! How you perform is a very important part of your legal reputation.

'Tricks of the trade': what barristers will try to do ...

When cross-examined do not be rigid or defensive. Keep your cool. Any lack of impartiality or overt advocacy will diminish the value of your evidence — if not make it worthless. It also goes against the Expert Code of Conduct in which your responsibility is to the court not the parties. Make every effort to be fair to both sides. As lawyers say there is 'no property in an expert witness'.

> Author comment
>> Bruce: The strength of your opinion is important. I have a graduated scale of concern from notable but not significant ('feather on the scales'), significant, clear concern, up to grave concern. Be careful and measured in offering opinion, for example with child drawings in the Family Court I would clearly distinguish what I think indicates level of attachment and speculative interpretation. Be careful with wild Freudian interpretations: 'Sometimes a cigar is just a cigar!' Barristers will constantly put pressure to either strengthen or diminish your conviction about a point (depending on whether it serves their client). Be precise about your strength of conviction — perhaps expressing it as a percentage, which I have found at times helpful to the court.

Watch the barrister who gives a sweeping generalisation, 'Wouldn't you agree that ...'. Respond with something like, 'I would agree with some aspects of what you have said, but I would make one or two qualifications. Would you like me to explain further?' On very rare occasions a barrister will try to force you to say yes or no to what is being put to you and I think it is appropriate to say 'mostly yes' or 'mostly no'. If this is not allowed then I would follow the advice of Phil Watts to say 'If I answer with a yes or no answer it would be misleading to the court'. An absolute fall back is to remind the barrister that you have just made an oath to give the 'whole truth and nothing but the truth'.

Barristers use a technique of 'closing the gate' that can lead you to a conclusion you do not want to make. This is only effective if you make or concede to generalisations, not if you qualify in the interests of accuracy every point you make. The barrister may say 'Wouldn't you agree that …'; I will say, 'No, I think it is more nuanced than that. I think that there are three issues, not one. Would you like me to repeat what I have said?'. I have often repeated what I have previously said and simply reinforced my evidence to the judge. If you get caught (being led somewhere you didn't want to go), simply admit to making too many generalisations and then refuse to agree to what now seems the logical conclusion.

> *Author comment*
> Bruce: *By way of illustration, imagine being asked by a barrister whether the floor of the courtroom looks flat. I would say, 'Well it looks flat to me but I would like to be sure in any evidence I give. I would use a level indicator and take readings there and there (indicate every section of the floor of the court)'.*

You will know when you are achieving this because the questions and your answers will start going around in circles. This is a good sign that you are not conceding anything. Usually at that point the judge will say something like, 'You have asked that question before and Dr Stevens has already answered it in a satisfactory way'. Score one for the expert!

A more subtle way of working is the more careful building of evidence around a core point — what will later be the argument put to the judge in closing submissions. This can seem like 'closing the gate', and if you accept any generalisations you will feel pressure to accept the barrister's 'logical' but simplistic conclusion. I actually think that this approach is very reasonable and need not distort your evidence if you are precise in giving your evidence. Accept that the barrister has a point but has not presented the whole picture.

If you feel pressured in the box, then it is a good idea to slow the proceedings down. If you feel swept along, pause and think before you answer. There is no rush and this will give an impression of deliberation about the expression of your opinion. If the barrister asks one or more questions in a question or it becomes convoluted, write the points down. I have put barristers on the spot by replying, 'You have asked me three questions, would you like me to answer them in sequence?'. It is not uncommon for them to get confused or forget part of a question.

Other evidence may have arisen in a trial and a barrister may want you to express an opinion on it (e.g., 'Would it change your recommendations about unsupervised contact if you had been informed that the father has been convicted of child sexual assault on three occasions?'). When this happens simply say 'Yes'. Never say that you had a different view of the father based on your clinical interview.

> In the Family Court a barrister in a contested residency case asked Mary, 'Would you change your opinion over the competence of the mother if you heard that she had left her children (aged 4 and 6) for five hours unsupervised at home while she went out drinking?'; Mary said, 'Yes'.

Initially I was impatient when barristers presented a scenario, thinking it was simply a mind game, until a leading family lawyer explained why it was important. I will now listen carefully, preface my response with something like 'I am to assume ...' and then give an opinion. If you need to pause and think through your response then do it. The court will wait and you will be seen as careful and considered in your opinion. If the suggested situation has no substance then the judge will simply ignore what you say. Remember to convey being *reasonable* and *flexible* as this shows that the 'scientist's mind is open' to new information.

> Author comment
>
> Bruce: I think it is helpful to the judge to be as transparent as possible about your logic. Outline A–B–C, not A–C (Watts, 2004). Never make guru-like pronouncements. Instead allow the train of your thought to be seen: 'I thought that this might be the case, but then ... I also checked ... and after weighing both conclusions, I thought ... 'I do this in my reports, so it is consistent to follow the same line in court. Avoid saying 'I feel' or 'I guess' — what is important is what you think. The basis is facts or theory.

The most difficult barrister is the one who has done his or her homework. This barrister knows you. He or she will have a game plan that is not obvious, more like the indirect tactics advocated by the famous military strategist Sun Tzu (1988). However you will generally not have any difficulties if you stay with careful and precise evidence, transparent logic and being completely non-defensive.

It is inevitable that something will happen (eventually) in which you feel embarrassed.

> Author comment
>
> Bruce: I remember an incident in which a legal secretary was taking notes. While I was speaking on the phone with her to arrange an appointment, I made a flippant remark that was later used by the barrister in cross-examination. I was non-defensive, 'took it on the chin' and to my surprise impressed the judge with my credibility.

The judge attaches considerable weight to the believability of the testimony, which is a skill they develop, and this applies to experts as well.

During the court recess, it is advisable not to talk openly about the proceedings in the public area, since you may not be aware of who is listening. Ask to go into a private room if necessary. DO NOT laugh about anything in the public area.

Even if you try everything and you feel like a flop after giving evidence, do not be too concerned. Every court appearance is a learning experience. We learn by making mistakes. This is unavoidable, since our opinion is never perfect. We do the best we can and what we have said is generally only a small part of the proceedings.

Conclusion: pressure on opinion

The most obvious pressure is from a solicitor or a party in a dispute. Usually this is more pronounced when our role is that of a 'hired gun' rather than a court appointed or agreed expert. It is important to be clear on the point that no matter who pays — 'our opinion is not for sale'. We sell our time not our opinion.

More subtle is internal pressure, what therapists call counter-transference, from our own history or personal issues. As an example, an assessor who suffered domestic violence (DV) as a child may overreact to violence cues and lose objectivity in an assessment.

We have to give up the myth that an expert can attain complete objectivity — as if we have a privileged observer role. Strong currents will swirl around and within, and we need to become aware and then make allowances. Objectivity is not something we assume we have, but something we strive for.

Chapter 11

Contingency planning

Money. Now that we have your attention, the following statement will not come as a surprise: You have to have more money 'coming in' than 'going out' to survive in private practice. You produce the income.

Usually when a practitioner begins in private practice they are in good health, motivated and want to get started. However, there are contingencies that you will need to consider. It is important to plan for the future — whatever may come.

Perhaps most psychologists enjoy their work and many will want to continue practising until well past the age of retirement. But you will be lucky to avoid any signs of declining health with increasing age. You should anticipate that at some point you may not be able to generate an income. Sound financial advice in early to mid-career can allow you to retire comfortably. The whole question of superannuation is too important to leave to later. Also, many psychologists dismiss or do not carefully consider the implications of both transient and serious illness, and how it impacts upon practice.

Reflect: Have you invested in financial advice? Do you set aside money for tax requirements and superannuation?

Contingency planning also includes thinking about insurance. There are life insurance and income protection options, lump sum payments on diagnosis of certain conditions, and ongoing payments when you are unable to work. Anyone in private practice should consider carefully having a review by a competent financial advisor to consider how best to manage risk. Such plans may be less expensive than you might imagine and can be a tax deduction.

There are additional contingency management strategies that are also important to consider. Have you made a will that specifies what to do with your medical records? What about a contingency plan, if for some reason you become incapable, is there a plan for the sharing of information with colleagues to enable appropriate continuation of treatment of your clients?

Think about your notes. We discussed this in a previous chapter but if you were not able to practice, would there be sufficient information for someone to continue with your cases?

Contingency management also considers the fact that external life events occur. In Australia there have been bushfires and floods that have destroyed psychologists' practices. Robbery, especially in city areas, can be a problem. If your computer or laptop is stolen is it password protected? Do you have a back-up copy of data? Does somebody have access to your financial records independent of your sole computer? In this day and age of cloud technology and portable back-up devices, a well-run practice has contingency systems for data in the event of both minor and major disruptions.

To Do:

Investigate professional services for the secure storage of your records. There does not seem to be a consensus about the use of cloud technology such as Drop Box, but this may be an option at some point in the future (with encryption).

There are ethical considerations in regard to being fit to practice. Essentially, to be a good therapist one needs to be reasonably alert (not overly tired). You need to able to focus and hold people's emotional information. If either you or someone close to you is going through a major trauma, turmoil or illness, this can impact upon performance. It is important to recognise early when your performance has been affected. The Australian Health Practitioner Regulation Agency (AHPRA) requires that we sign a declaration to indicate being physically capable of doing the job and if you fall below that standard, ethically you have a responsibility to stop.

Denial is common after a person is diagnosed with major illness. There is a resistance to recognising or acknowledging that my performance is 'slipping'. It is important to discuss this with your colleagues. This would be a time to seek help if you are overwhelmed emotionally.

Reflect: Do you have a peer group for supervision, or an individual supervisor? Do you feel free to discuss personal issues? Have you ever been in therapy? It is important that in a time of unusual stress that you seek treatment well before it becomes a 'last resort'.

Author comment
Phil: In the 25 years I have worked in private practice I have suffered a major motor vehicle accident and my wife has twice been diagnosed with cancer. These are very significant life events that, at the time, impacted on my performance. Fortunately, one of the options I had in my practice was to cease doing therapy and continue only with assessment. Assessment requires less emotional commitment. I also sought professional counselling to ensure that I could manage the emotions through some of the more difficult periods.

Career planning

There are two universal forces at work in running a practice: the Yin and the Yang. The first principle is that success follows good planning and setting goals. As psychologists we have good research skills. These can be applied to developing a good business plan.

> *Author comment*
>
> *Phil: I believe in planning. However, planning has two distinct disadvantages. The world does not always cooperate, and it is possible that if someone is too focused on a plan then opportunities might be missed. The principle of serendipity is likely to shape your business and future career more than the plans you make. I graduated with a Clinical Masters. At the time I graduated I did not know what forensic psychology was, nor would I have chosen a career in that area. However, in 1989 the WA economy collapsed. There was a freeze on hiring in the public service, and the only position I could get was an Essential Service item that translated as a Psychologist in a Juvenile Remand Centre. Twenty-five years later, approximately 10% of my income is in clinical psychology and 90% in forensic psychology.*

Therefore, serendipity of life, opportunities and circumstance will shape the direction your practice takes. However, success is not completely random and there are some principles that will shape your career. You would be well advised to work hard to be the best you can be within your area of expertise. Clients expect you to have good clinical skills, ensuring that you are trained in a variety of effective techniques and are frequently updating your skills. It is also essential to have good interpersonal skills with those you treat.

Sources of referral

GPs keep a number of factors in mind. These involve key words such as 'efficiency', 'quality', 'reliability', and 'availability'.

> *Author comment*
>
> *Phil: It never ceases to amaze me how psychologists in private practice do not understand the need to quickly and efficiently prepare reports, to make themselves available for services, and to respond to the needs of the referrers. Most psychologists find that the majority of their work comes from a handful of sources. It is important to nurture those sources.*

Make yourself useful and known to the referral sources in your clinical area. If you sent letters to one hundred GPs it may not be as effective as a face-to-face visit to GPs in a practice. It is important to network. Therefore, a psychologist should understand where GPs meet for information and training, such as through their local network, and which magazines they actually read. You might think about an advertisement. Remember that writing articles for GP magazines is a good way of showing your expertise to potential referrers. But having said all this, one of the best sources of referral is existing clients.

> *Reflect: When did you last seek professional assistance? How did you select the professional to help you? For example, if you wanted legal advice, how would you select a lawyer? If you can identify the steps, what does it say about the way in which someone might find you?*

> *Author comment*
>
> *Bruce: For years I wrote articles for Australian Doctor. It was helpful in developing my practice long before*

> Medicare rebated psychologists. Self-help books for
> couples also helped.

Friend or foe?

There are not many places in Australia where you could set
up a practice without there being existing services. If you set
up a practice, it is worth thinking about how you will relate
to existing practices. Will they consider you 'competition'
and a threat?

> *Author comment*
>
> *Phil: When I set up practice in my area I made a point
> of going to visit existing practitioners. I tried to meet
> with them for lunch every 4 to 6 weeks to provide
> professional support and a cross-section of referrals
> within each other's areas of expertise. I doubt if there
> was any diminishing of market-share, and it seemed
> that everyone benefitted from mutual support.*

Networking is an essential skill for private practitioners. There
are bodies of independent private practitioners, Australian
Psychological Society (APS) interest groups, and colleges with
conferences and other professional development activities. You
may be tempted to think that spending time being involved in
professional organisations will be counterproductive to
building your practice. However, this does not recognise that
professional networks are an important source of referral and
support, especially when you encounter difficult cases.

> *Author comment*
>
> *Phil: It was only through informal networks that I
> learned how to self-publish a book (the first of many).
> It was also how I became an Adjunct Associate
> Professor at Canberra University. At the end of the day
> it was my ability that enabled me to achieve both of*

those tasks, but it was through being known to other people that I was able to enlist their support and, when opportunities arose, they thought of me. Consequently, successful practitioners ensure that they network widely.

Being active in various organisations allows people to get to know you. Such roles create very important networking opportunities. For example, after organising an event on Criminal Injuries Compensation reports, I became friends with the Chief Assessor of Criminal Injuries WA because of the association started solely through professional contact.

Professional development

You will naturally want to update your skills within your own area of expertise. However, it is equally important to occasionally do training in areas completely outside your practice area. This ensures a wide knowledge base. It also leads to new contacts. This creates a very important professional network across a wide range of skills.

Opportunities and diversification

'Psychology 101' teaches us a core principle: habituation. If you apply this to your career you will find that when you first began to practice you are quite over-aroused because every client is a new client. Over time seeing clients becomes familiar and our confidence grows. After about five years of practice, most clients coming through the door are representative of types of conditions with which we are familiar. Rather than be overwhelmed, we slip into a routine. However, if we continue on that path it gradually reaches a point where our interest diminishes. Unless you reinvent yourself, or diversify interests and activities, the work that you enjoy now may well become something of a 'millstone around your neck'.

There are a variety of ways to diversify. Think about the diversifying your practice. You might stay within your area of expertise, but extend to new areas of interest. For example, if you conduct therapy with adults, do training in child therapy and extend your repertoire. If you work with depression and anxiety, pick on a new area of interest such as treating addictions, or relationship therapy.

One of the fundamental limitations as a therapist is that your income is tied to your face-to-face interaction with a person. This limits the amount of income you can generate and the number of lives you can touch. Therefore, there are a variety of additional ways to diversify which can be rewarding and interesting.

You might think about doing workshops or training courses in psychology, where professional development is a requirement.

> *Author comment*
>
> *Phil: In the last few years there has been an oversupply of training. Attendance numbers on average are diminishing, but there is still opportunity. Consider the maths at 2015 rates: 30 people attending a training course at $300 each — take out 40% for costs, and you can produce $5,000 for a day's work. At Medicare rates one would have to see 50 people for the same income. You can arrange your own workshops, taking the risks yourself and this can produce significant rewards.*

If you are considering offering training, there are other options. You can do professional development training within the profession. Obviously, you will need an area of competency to share with other psychologists. However, running short training courses, such as topics for the community, may improve referral bases and improve your competence in running the training. It is also rewarding to help touch lives through sharing information.

New technology is changing the face of the training landscape. Webinars can be broadcast globally. If you provide special topics, then Webinars are a low cost way of establishing a training presence.

It is satisfying to write books. You may feel that this is a task that is too daunting to be able to achieve, but start small by writing articles on psychology for your local paper. This will also advertise your practice: a win-win.

> *Author comment*
>
> *Phil: I have found that the easiest way to write a book is to buy a dictaphone and dictate the words. One of my colleagues suggested taping one of my day-long workshops, and then having it transcribed — this formed the basis of the book. Once a book has been dictated, you have the option of self-publishing (and there are plenty of courses and information on how to do it) or approaching a publisher. To self-publish a hard copy book used to cost between $5,000 and $10,000 for 2,000 copies. With rapidly growing technology it is quite easy and affordable to produce eBooks. Companies such as Pickawoowoo can assist with all stages of book production including cover design, layout, eBook setup, as well as set you up for online sales. Currently the cost is approximately $2,000, with books printed on demand.*

A book can touch lives.

> *Author coment*
>
> *Bruce: In 2000 I wrote Mirror, mirror: When self-love undermines your relationship. This sold 4,000 copies in Australia and I still get requests for it. I am pleased*

> *that it has helped many people over the years to better understand difficult relationships. I have just completed an eBook called Emotional learning: The way we are wired for intimacy (released through Fontaine Press), which is self-published.*

A book that sells well is generally sold independently of whether or not you are working. Therefore, it value-adds income. If it is on a topic related to something in which you train or conduct therapy, it may also generate clients and sales at workshops.

Another type of diversification is to look for jobs that other people do not particularly like. For example, in Western Australia it is hard to get people to do country assessments.

> **Author comment**
> *Phil: I actually enjoy taking on a country assessment because it takes me out of the office for a day or two. Sometimes I take my wife or family with me, and we have a micro-holiday around me conducting an assessment. The diversified activity makes the task enjoyable.*

In private practice, doing research can also be beneficial. If you would like to do research it is probably wise to take the collaborative approach. You might seek people in a university who have access to the data, and you can become involved in developing ideas. By collaborating, nobody does all the work but it lifts your credibility as an expert if you have published material within your topic area.

Try to predict trends in your profession and community. See if you can identify the 'hot' areas. If you are alert to this and by understanding, promoting, and getting training or offering training in such areas you can have a diversified practice.

> Author comment
> Phil: I identified a clinical need to treat people with sexual addiction, especially internet pornography. This led to the book Internet pornography: Do-it-yourself treatment guide for men, published in 2014.

Making money

There are many emotional rewards in being a psychologist. We can help someone change their life or overcome life problems. But ultimately as a psychologist, in private practice, we are a business. It is essential to understand that you are entitled to be paid for the services rendered. This realisation should come early! Psychologists are often 'too nice' and undervalue what they do.

> Author comment
> Phil: Ask any private practitioner and you will hear a familiar story. Someone comes for therapy, puts forward a very good case of not having enough money to pay your full rate, so you heavily discount the therapy session. After 8 sessions she then announces she is not going to coming for the next four weeks because she is going for an overseas holiday.

Such experiences help us to understand that we are entitled to reimbursement. It is important to carefully consider your fee structure. The APS recommends a standard hourly fee recommended for all psychologists, irrespective if someone has done four or six years' training, whether they have worked for 5 or 25 years, and whether they have specialist expertise or not. In an area such as law, new graduates charge at one rate, experienced solicitors at another, barristers at another, and Senior Counsel charge at another rate again. Therefore, it is up to us to follow the fine print on the APS fee structure that states psychologists can charge whatever they like (which is in keeping with the anti-competitive legislation).

When you first start out you will probably take on whatever work you can. This is fine. Both you and your market are working out what you are good at. Usually work will increase. However, once your practice is established it is important to do a cost-benefit analysis of what you do.

> *Author comment*
>> *Phil: As a Clinical and Forensic Psychologist I have people coming for therapy and I also have assessments. There was a point approximately 10 years ago where I was excessively busy and, as a result, I sought advice from a colleague (co-author Bruce Stevens) and his advice was 'If you're too busy put your fees up'. Ultimately I did, and this seemed to just generate more work. A few years after that, it then became important to do another cost-benefit analysis. My wife was sick, and I wanted to reduce the hours I was working. I analysed all of the costs associated with my activities. For example, in a therapy session if you consider how many 'no-shows' there are, how long it takes to write a GP Mental Health report and so forth, I found that therapy was one of my least profitable items. On the other hand, I found that in doing short assessments I was able to charge top dollar with the lowest costs. Therefore, over time I have reduced therapy and increased assessments.*

A business principle that is well recognised is to do what you do best and pay people to do the menial tasks. While we understand the costs associated with having a secretary or receptionist, a receptionist might work for a rate of $25 an hour whereas you may be able to earn $200 an hour. If a receptionist can save you one hour in a day, they have more than paid for themselves.

Rather than thinking of full-time staff, also look at different contract arrangements. Some secretarial services will answer phones.

Author comment
Phil: I use two typists to whom I provide dictated reports to type, and therefore they do it on a sub-contract basis. It is important, however, to ensure that any contract staff sign privacy agreements to respect client privacy and not release information.

Writing reports yourself can be quite slow. Learning to use a dictaphone and having somebody type it, and sometimes even learning how to use a voice-to-text programme, can be a significant cost-saver over time.

Author comment
Bruce: I have always trained graduate students. Over the years I was helped by students administering and scoring tests. They sit in with my assessment and help to write the report (from my written notes).
Sometimes a student will do a literature or file review and do home visits. I will pay them for their work at a reasonable rate.

Many successful practices will make money by renting rooms to other psychologists. This can be better than setting up business arrangements and cost sharing. Therefore, if you have a large flow of business into your practice and are in the position of renting office space, ensure that there is a spare room that you can sub-lease to a colleague.

Author comment

> Phil: I have two consulting rooms in my current office, one sub-leased to a colleague and the second one was requested by someone who wanted to do Saturday work. I do not work on a Saturday, so the rent assistance helps.

> Bruce: I have nine offices in a building in the Canberra CBD. All are rented out with psychologists in private practice. There is a very modest profit on office rent alone. There are huge benefits in being surrounded by highly skilled colleagues.

It is also important to remember that being satisfied with yourself will not simply come from money. It is also important to ensure that you maintain some pro-bono or charity work, remember the poor and afflicted, to ensure that you meet their needs.

Author comment

> Bruce: I will bulk bill about 30% of my consultations. This is because I often see sex offenders who cannot get employment. While bulk billing as a clinical psychologist has a better return than for generalists, it is below my normal fee. The Australian Government has used the Better Access initiative to provide more widely available psychological services, so it is up to me to do what I can.

Enjoy what you do

Variety is the spice of life. So to maintain a practice for 10, 20, 30 or more years it is important to ensure that there is plenty of variety to prevent burnout and enjoy the journey. Habituation means that you will become bored with the things that you do year-in, year-out. Change is good.

Author comment

> Phil: I have been able to reinvent myself at least three times within my career. There are a number of practical things that can be done to make private practice enjoyable. As a private practitioner I believe that having a varied work life, ensuring that you diversify between therapy, assessment, training, group therapy, and other areas of practice will maximise a range of enjoyment. It is important to find contracts with government departments and so forth, where you take on different roles in different areas. With experience, giving supervision also becomes an option.

Psychologists are required to do professional development training. Stepping out of a practice and doing a training day is quite beneficial. However, think outside of the square by choosing interstate training and coupling it with a short holiday. You might think of such holidays as 'power breaks' where the period may only be for 3 or 4 days, but it steps you out of your routine. Because it is linked to training days there are tax deductable benefits.

If you think about holidays one of the advantages of remaining a government employee is four weeks annual leave. In private practice, leaving your practice for three weeks might be difficult because of the impact on cash flow. Consequently, most practitioners take a series of short breaks rather than one long holiday. Therefore, identify different periods over the year to take holidays. Coupling holidays with public holidays also allows you to get maximum time off with minimum lost income. Consider adding a few days leave to a gazetted public holiday, which may extend the break to possibly five or six days

Think about your daily routine. If you do only therapy then it is a good idea to take a lunch break and get outside of the office for at least 30 to 45 minutes. This will help to clear your head and reset your mind.

Psychologists teach the benefits of doing exercise. You need to apply the same rule for yourself. It is important to keep yourself fit, because most of what you do is quite sedentary, either sitting in therapy or sitting at the computer. Therefore, keep yourself fit and structure moments of energetic activity during the day.

A strategy to help enjoy what you do is to take control of your diary. If you give people unlimited choice, your diary will look a little like Swiss cheese with gaps and holes all through it. Ideally, what you need to do is have blocks of time and narrow the clients into certain times. While on the subject of diaries, I recommend using an electronic diary system that includes automatic SMS features. They are modestly priced (less than $100 a month) but these features allow you and your staff to access the diary at any time. It also improves attendance by sending reminders.

> *Author comment*
>> Phil: I have a mixed practice that allows me more opportunity to do different things. However, the way I have structured my practice for a long time was to do therapy in the afternoon and assessment in the morning. That way, if I had to go to court to give evidence I already have the mornings, where I only have to move one appointment (instead of three or four to move in the afternoon). I also look for opportunities to work away from the office so that I am not sitting at my desk every day.
>> One of the advantages of working for yourself is flexibility. If you see clients in the evening, make sure that

you take some time off during the day to allow the benefits associated with having some flexibility.

Fit to Practice

Chapter 12

To close a practice (and sell it if you can)

Selling your practice

As the baby boomers reach retirement age, many of us are asking the question: What is my practice worth?'. The age old reply will be: 'Whatever someone is prepared to pay!'.

The Australian Psychological Society (APS) has prepared a guide to this issue that was produced in March 2014 — *Selling or closing your practice: A practice guide for psychologists*[1] (see www.psychology.org.au).

The guide addresses some of the key tasks regarding selling or closing a practice, such as notifying staff, notifying clients, obtaining a valuation, record keeping and storage obligations and insurances required.

We would add to this some further notes of caution: the method of selling or closing a practice is dependent on the original business structure you set up. For example, if you used your name as a sole trader or as a 'trading as' arrangement then the practice may be difficult to sell without the structure of a proprietary limited company ('Pty Ltd') that

---

1 https://www.psychology.org.au/Assets/Files/Selling-Practice_Guide_for_Psychologists.pdf

owns the business. If you are a sole trader who has contractors working for you, they may not agree to being 'sold' with the business. Their contract may be with you and not transferable.

You may own the property and/or the fixtures such as furniture, computers, and test library, which are more easily valued and sold. You need to think about it from the point of view of the buyer: why would they want to buy your practice? Is the practice saleable due to the referral base, its location and phone number and/or the fact that your practice has been there for some years and is therefore known to local GPs?

If you have worked in your practice with others, you have effectively worked for the fees and income you have generated along the way (effectively a wage) and possibly not much more unless a bigger practice wants to buy your practice. Usually in these arrangements, there is an expectation that you would stay on for a certain period of time and the payment for the sale may be in instalments over that time (commonly known as an 'earn out').

The other way in which a practice may have to be closed can be due to the ill health of the practice owner. If you are operating a practice on your own or with others, it is important to have in place instructions as to how the practice might be wound up if you were to become too ill to operate the business, or meet an untimely death. These are not pleasant subjects but need to be broached with your accountant and be part of the instructions for winding up or transferring your practice if you are not there to oversee such a process. The American Psychological Association (APA) recommends the establishment of a 'professional will'[2] that essentially designates a 'professional executor' who carries out your wishes

---

2 http://apapracticecentral.org/update/2014/06-26/professional-will.aspx

and instructions should your practice have to be closed in your absence (see http://apapracticecentral.org).

The APS has a similar guide[3] (see www.psychology.org.au) that notes a practice contingency plan is desirable:

> The APS recommends that psychologists in independent practice prepare a Practice Contingency Plan to support the management of their business in the event of their death or incapacitation. A Practice Contingency Plan is not the same as a Will, does not have the same legal standing as a Will and is not intended to be a legally binding document. It is intended to be a 'guide' or a 'plan' that offers an immediate way forward to assist the Executor of the Will in the expeditious management of practice affairs in the event of a psychologist's untimely death. Some key aspects of a practice contingency plan include:
>
> • identification of a professional nominee who can conduct the formal closing of the business;
> • office information and security arrangements;
> • location of client records and contact details;
> • instructions for notifying clients; and
> • details of professional indemnity insurance. (APS, p.1)

Issues that need to be taken into account where a practice has to be closed down quickly are:

• Storage of files — scanning and 'cloud' storage is an increasingly popular option rather than establishing storage for paper files. These files need to be accessible regardless and a method of doing so established whether you are around or not. Files need to finalised in a way that is consistent with the Health Records Act in your state and any advice you can obtain from appropriate authorities regarding your responsibilities to current and former clients.

• Business responsibilities in winding up of the practice includes debts, taxation, superannuation and leave entitlements for staff be paid out, finalisation of agreements

---

3 https://www.psychology.org.au/Assets/Files/Guidelines-death-of-psychologist.pdf

with contractors, finalising tax returns, GST and BAS payments and notification of closing or transfer of the business to the appropriate authorities.

- What should happen to books, resources, tests and other items related to psychological practice?

- The Professional Practice Will is a useful document to have prepared in case of incapacitation or death. The document expresses your wishes for the practice and how the task of winding up a practice can be undertaken by a designated colleague rather than it falling to a family member (Barnett, Zimmerman, & Walfish, 2014)

The biggest difficulty with this subject is that much of what psychologists are doing about selling or winding up practices is done almost secretively and somewhat furtively. There is limited information available to assist us that is psychology-specific and there are limited advisors (accountants and lawyers) who specialise in private allied health practices or more specifically psychology practices.

The *American Counseling Association guide to selling practices*[4] (2005; see http://www.counseling.org) notes that the process should be commenced two years prior to the desired selling point. A cursory perusal of the internet via Google shows that there are very few psychology practices for sale in Australia that are listed with a broker. Only one site had an indicative price and it was hard to work out what the price was based on income or assets or valuation.

Reflect: What value would you place on your practice? It is probably worth less than you think. Why would anyone buy it if they could simply rent an office, approach local GPs and

---

4 See http://www.counseling.org/docs/private-practice-ointers/selling_or_buying_a_private_practice.pdf?sfvrsn=2

soon build their own practice? Skilled psychologists soon have full books.

Planning is essential. This includes all those areas such as to sell or close your practice; or in case of illness or death, have your practice wound up by others if you are not able to. You owe it to yourself and your clients to have such a process in place; however, this type of forward planning is often over-looked by private practitioners because of the pressure of day-to-day business activities.

References

Chapter One

Department of Health. (2012, December). *Medicare benefits schedule — allied health services*. Canberra, ACT: Author.

Crago, H. (2013). Psychotherapy: The view from psychology. *Psychotherapy in Australia, 19*(4), 68–71.

Fletcher, J., King, K., Pirkis, J., Burgess, P., Blashki, G., Kohn, F., ... Reifels, L. (2011). Evaluating the access to allied psychological services component of the Better Outcomes in Mental Health Care program. Melbourne, Victoria: Centre for Health Policy, Programs and Economics, Melbourne School of Population Health, The University of Melbourne.

Grenyer, B.F., & Lewis, K.L. (2012). Prevalence, prediction, and prevention of psychologist misconduct. *Australian Psychologist, 47*(2), 68–76.

Health Practitioner Regulation National Law (Victoria) Act 2009

O'Donovan, A., Casey, L., Van der Veen, M., & Boschen, M. (2013). *Psychotherapy: An Australian perspective*. East Hawthorn, Victoria: IP Communications.

Prochaska, J.O., Norcross, J.C., & Krebs, P.M. (2011). Stages of change. *Journal of Clinical Psychology: In Session, 67*(2), 143–154.

Psychology Board of Australia. (2014, December). Registrant data. Retrieved from http://www.psychologyboard.gov.au/About/Statistics.aspx

Chapter Two

Australian Psychological Society. (2014). *Models of private practice: A private practice guide for psychologists*. Retrieved from https://www.psychology.org.au/practitioner/resources/

Barnett, J.E., Zimmerman, J., & Walfish, S. (2014). *The ethics of private practice: A practical guide for mental health professionals.* New York, NY: Oxford University Press.

Beck, A.T., & Steer, R.A. (1993). *Beck Anxiety Inventory manual.* San Antonio, TX: Psychological Corporation.

Beck, A.T., Steer, R.A., & Brown, G.K. (1996). *Manual for the Beck Depression Inventory-II.* San Antonio, TX: Psychological Corporation.

Ben-Porath, Y.S., & Tellegen, A. (2008/2011). *MMPI-2-RF (Minnesota Multiphasic Personality Inventory-2 Restructured Form): Manual for administration, scoring, and interpretation.* Minneapolis, MN: University of Minnesota Press.

Briere, J. (1995). *Trauma Symptom Inventory professional manual.* Lutz, FL: Psychological Assessment Resources.

Butcher, J.N., Dahlstrom, W.G., Graham, J.R., Tellegen, A.M., & Kreammer, B. (1989). *The Minnesota Multiphasic Personality Inventory-2 (MMPI-2) Manual for Administration and Scoring.* Minneapolis, MN: University of Minneapolis Press.

Garner, D.M. (2004). *Eating Disorder Inventory–3: Professional Manual.* Lutz FL: Psychological Assessment Resources.

Goodman, R. (1997). The Strengths and Difficulties Questionnaire: A research note. *Journal of Child Psychology and Psychiatry, 38,* 581–586.

Grodzki, L. (2000). *Building your ideal private practice: A guide for therapists and other healing professionals.* New York, NY: W.W. Norton.

Holland, J.L. (1994). *Self-directed search.* Lutz, FL: Psychological Assessment Resources.

Jensen, M.P., Turner, J.A., Romano, J.M., & Strom, S.E. (1995). The Chronic Pain Coping Inventory: Development and preliminary validation. *Pain, 60,* 203–216.

Knowdell, R.L. (2002a). *Career Values Card Sort.* San Jose, CA: Career Research & Testing.

Knowdell, R.L. (2002b). *Motivated Skills Card Sort.* San Jose, CA: Career Research & Testing.

Knowdell, R.L. (2002c). *Occupational Interests Card Sort.* San Jose, CA: Career Research & Testing.

Linder, H., & Stokes, D. (2007), Survey of psychologists providing Medicare services under Better Access to Mental Health Care. *In Psych: The Bulletin of the Australian Psychological Society Ltd., 29*(5). 30-31. Retrieved August 6, 2014, from https://www.psychology.org.au/inpsych/survey_medicare/

Lovibond, S.H., & Lovibond, P.F. (1995). *Manual for the Depression Anxiety Stress Scales* (2nd. ed.) Sydney, NSW: Psychology Foundation.

Miller, S.D., & Bargmann, S. (2012). The Outcome Rating Scale (ORS) and the Session Rating Scale (SRS). *Integrating Science and Practice, 2*(2), 28–31. Retrieved from https://www.ordrepsy.qc.ca/en/documentation-et-medias/integrating-science-and-practice.sn

Millon, T., Millon, C., Davis, R., & Grossman, S. (2009). *MCMI-III Manual* (4th ed.). Minneapolis, MN: Pearson Education.

Morey, L.C. (2007). *The Personality Assessment Inventory professional manual.* Lutz, FL: Psychological Assessment Resources.

Norcross, J.C. (2013). *Self-help that works: Resources to improve emotional health and strengthen relationships* (4th ed.). New York, NY: Oxford University Press.

Russell, M.T., & Karol, D. (2002). *The 16PF Fifth Edition administrator's manual.* Champaign, IL: Institute for Personality and Ability Testing.

Shaw, E., & Breckenridge, J. (2014). Reciprocal Influences: Exploring the intertwining identities of therapist and mother. *Psychotherapy in Australia, 20*(4), 30–39.

Stokes, D., Mathews, R., Grenyer, B.F.S., & Crea, K. (2010). The Australian psychology workforce 3: A national profile of psychologists in salaried employment or in independent private practice. *Australian Psychologist, 45*, 178–188.

Stone, B.A. (2004). *Pictured Feelings Instrument: A nonverbal vocabulary of feelings*. Melbourne, Vic: Australian Council for Educational Research (ACER).

Weathers, F.W., Litz, B.T., Herman, D.S., Huska, J.A., & Keane, T.M. (1993). *The PTSD Checklist (PCL): Reliability, validity, and diagnostic utility*. Paper presented at the 9th Annual Conference of the ISTSS, San Antonio, TX.

Young, J.E., & Brown, G. (1994). Young Schema Questionnaire. In J. E. Young (Ed.), *Cognitive therapy for personality disorders: A schema-focused approach* (2nd ed.). Sarasota, FL: Professional Resource Press.

Young, J.E., Arntz, A., Atkinson, T., Lobbestael, J., Weishaar, M.E., van Vreeswijk, M.F., & Klokman, J. (2007). *The Schema Mode Inventory*. New York, NY: Schema Therapy Institute.

Chapter Three

Compliance. (n.d.). In Oxford's online dictionary. Retrieved from http://www.oxforddictionaries.com/definition/english/compliance

Health Services Group. (2012). *Clinical framework for the delivery of health services*. Victorian WorkCover Authority. Retrieved from http://www.vwa.vic.gov.au/__data/assets/pdf_file/0006/3885/clinical-framework.pdf

Mathews, R. (2011). Medicare compliance audits: An update. *In Psych, 33*(6), 26. Retrieved from http://www.psychology.org.au/InPsych2011/Medicare-compliance-audits/

Mathews, R. (2014). How to … prepare for a PsyBA audit. *In Psych, 36*(1), 27. Retrieved from http://www.psychology.org.au/Content.aspx?ID=5679

Pastore, T. (2013). *The anxiety of psychological practice in Australia or surviving in private practice*. Bloomington, IN: XLIBRIS

Shaw, E. (2014) Sacred cows and sleeping dogs: Beating burnout [online]. *Psychotherapy in Australia, 20* (2), 64–65.

Chapter Four

Arntz, A., & Jacob, G. (2013). *Schema therapy in practice: An introductory guide to the schema mode approach.* Oxford: Wiley-Blackwell.

Beck, J.S. (2011). *Cognitive behavior therapy: Basics and beyond* (2nd ed.). New York, NY: Guilford Press.

Berman, Pearl (2014). *Case conceptualization and treatment planning: Integrating theory with clinical practice.* (Revised ed.) LA: Sage.

Burrows, G.D., Stanley, R., & Bloom, P.B. (2001). *International handbook of clinical hypnosis.* Chichester: Wiley.

Cabaniss, D.L. (2011). *Psychodynamic psychotherapy a clinical manual.* Chichester, West Sussex, England: Wiley-Blackwell.

de Shazer, S., Dolan, Y., Korman, H., Trepper, T., McCollum, E., & Berg, I.K., Steve (2007). *More than miracles: The state of the art of Solution-focused Brief Therapy.* New York, NY: Routledge.

Elliott, R., Watson, J.C., Goldman, R.N., & Greenberg, L.S. (2004). *Learning Emotion-focused Therapy: The process-experiential approach to change.* Washington, DC: American Psychological Association.

Hayes, S.C., Strosahl, K., & Wilson, K.G. (1999). *Acceptance and Commitment Therapy: An experiential approach to behavior change.* New York, NY: Guilford Press.

Norcross, J.C., & Lambert, M.J. (2013). Compendium of evidence-based relationships. *Psychotherapy in Australia, 19*(3), 34–37.

North, M.M., North, S.M., & Coble, J.R. (1996). *Virtual Reality Therapy: An innovative paradigm.* Colorado Springs: IPI Press.

Ryle, A., & Kerr, I. (2002). *Introducing cognitive analytic therapy: Principles and practice.* Chichester, England: Wiley.

Segal, Z.V., Williams, J.M. G., & Teasdale, J.D. (2002). *Mindfulness-Based Cognitive Therapy for depression: A new approach to preventing relapse.* New York, NY: Guilford Press.

Shapiro, F. (2001). *Eye movement desensitization and reprocessing: Basic principles, protocols, and procedures* (2nd ed.). New York, NY: Guilford Press.

Summers, R.F., & Barber, J.P. (2010). *Psychodynamic Therapy: A guide to evidence-based practice.* New York, NY: Guilford Press.

Weissman, M.M, Markowitz, J.C., & Klerman, G.L. (2007). *Clinician's quick guide to interpersonal psychotherapy.* New York: Oxford University Press.

Weerasekera, P. (1996). *Multiperspective case formulation: A step towards treatment integration.* Melbourne, Victoria: Krieger.

Young, J.E., Klosko, J.S., & Weishaar, M.E. (2003). *Schema Therapy: A practitioner's guide.* New York, NY: Guilford Press.

Chapter Five

Carroll, M. (2013). Brain-based supervision. *Psychotherapy in Australia, 20*(1), 28–36.

Counselman, E. (2013). In consultation, peer supervision groups that work: Three steps that make a difference. *Psychotherapy Networker, 37*(3).

Crago, H. (2013). Straight talk on training, Psychotherapy: The view from psychology. *Psychotherapy in Australia, 19*(4), 68–71.

Kahneman, D. (2011). *Thinking fast and slow.* London: Allen Lane.

May, A. (2007). *Flip the switch.* Surry Hills, NSW: Messenger.

Watkins, C.E., & Milne, D.L. (2014) (Eds.) *Handbook of clinical supervision.* New York, NY: Wiley.

Chapter Six

Australian Health Practitioners Regulation Authority (AHRPA). Annual Report 2013–2014. *Regulating health practitioners: Managing risk to the public.*

Australian Psychological Society. (2007). *Code of ethics*. Melbourne, Victoria: Author.

Brennan, C. (2013). Ensuring ethical practice: Guidelines for mental health counsellors in private practice.*Journal of Mental Health Counseling, 35(3)*, *245–261.*

Shaw, E., Bancroft, H., Metzer, J., & Symonds, M. (2013). How to make an ethically sound decision. *Inpsych.* Retrieved from https://www.psychology.org.au/publications/inpsych/2013#dec201

Chapter Seven

Behary, W. (2013). *Disarming the narcissist: Surviving and thriving with the self-absorbed.* (2nd ed.). Oakland, CA: New Harbinger.

Covey, S.R. (2004). *The seven habits of highly effective people: Powerful lessons in personal change.* New York, NY: Free Press.

Figley, Charles R. (1995). Compassion fatigue: Toward a new understanding of the costs of caring. In B. Stamm & Hudnall (Eds). (1995). *Secondary traumatic stress: Self-care issues for clinicians, researchers, and* educators (pp. 3–28). Baltimore, MD, US: The Sidran Press

Fonagy, P., Gergely, G., Jurist, E., & Target, M. (2004). *Affect regulation, mentalization and the development of the self.* London, England: Karnac.

Hare, R. (1993). *Without conscience: The disturbing world of the psychopaths among us.* New York, NY: Guilford Press.

Hare, R. (2003). *Hare Psychopathy Checklist Revised (PCL-R).* (2nd ed.). Cheektowaga, NY: MHS.

MacLean, P. (1990). *The triune brain in evolution.* New York, NY: Plenum Press.

McWilliams, N. (2011). *Psychoanalytic diagnosis: Understanding personality structure in the clinical process.* (2nd ed.). New York, NY: Guilford.

Norcross, J., & Guy, J. (2007). *Leaving it at the office: A guide to psychotherapist self-care.* New York, NY: Guilford Press.

Chapter Eight

Bargmann, S., & Robinson, B. (2012). *Feedback-informed treatment (FIT) — Manual 2: Feedback-informed clinical work: The basics.* Chicago, IL: International Center for Clinical Excellence.

Bertolino, B., Axsen, R., Maeschalck, C., Miller, S.D., Babbins-Wagner, R. (2012). *Feedback-informed treatment (FIT) — Manual 6: Implementing feedback-informed work in agencies and systems of care.* Chicago, IL: International Center for Clinical Excellence.

Bertolino, B., Bargmann, S., & Miller, S.D. (2012). *Feedback-informed treatment (FIT) — Manual 1: What works in therapy: A primer.* Chicago, IL: International Center for Clinical Excellence.

Maeschalck, C., Bargmann, S., Miller, S.D, & Bertolino, B. (2012). *Feedback-informed treatment (FIT) — Manual 3: Feedback-informed supervision.* Chicago, IL: International Center for Clinical Excellence.

Miller et al, (2011). *Feedback-informed treatment* (FIT Manuals).

Miller, S., Hubble, M., & Duncan, B. (2007) Supershrinks: What is the secret of their success *Psychotherapy Networker, (November /December) p. 27–56.*

Minami, T., Wampold, B., Serlin, R., Hamilton, E., Brown, G., & Kircher, J. (2008). Benchmarking for psychotherapy efficacy. *Journal of Consulting and Clinical Psychology, 75,* 232–243.

Seide, J., & Miller, S.D. (2012). *Feedback-informed treatment (FIT) — Manual 4: Documenting dhange: A primer on measurement, analysis, and reporting.* Chicago, IL: International Center for Clinical Excellence.

Tilsen, J., Maeschalck, C., Seidel, J., Robinson, B., & Miller, S.D. (2012). *Feedback-informed treatment (FIT) — Manual 5: Feedback-informed clinical work: Specific populations and service settings.* Chicago, IL: International Center for Clinical Excellence.

Wampold, B.E. (2001). *The great psychotherapy debate: Models, methods and findings.* Mahwah, NJ: Lawrence Erlbaum.

Wampold, B.E., Imel, Z.E., Laska, K., Benish, S., Miller, S.D., Fluckiger, C., Del re, A.C., Baardseth, T.P., & Budge, S. (2010) Determining what works in the treatment of PTSD. *Clinical Psychology Review, 30,* 923–933.

Chapter Nine

Australian Psychological Society (APS). (2010). *How should client records be handled?* Retrieved from www.psychology.org.au

Berman, P. (2014). *Case conceptualization and treatment planning: Integrating theory with clinical practice.* (Rev. ed.). Thousand Oaks, CA: Sage.

Bradford, L., & Stevens, B. (2013). What's in the file? Opening the drawer on clinical record keeping in psychology. *Australian Psychologist, 48,* 178–187.

Harris, S.M., Brown, A., Dakin, J.B., Lucas, B., Riley, L., & Bulham, R. (2009). Are clinical records really that important? The dearth of research and practice guidelines in MFT literature. *American Journal of Family Therapy, 37*(5), 373–387.

Jenkins, P. (2003). Therapist responses to requests for disclosure of therapeutic records: An introductory study. *Counselling and Psychotherapy Research, 3*(3), 232–238.

King, R. (2010). Record keeping in psychotherapy. *Psychotherapy in Australia, 16*(3), 60–63.

Ladd, C. (1967). Record-keeping and research in psychiatric and psychological clinics. *Journal of Counselling Psychology, 14*(4), 361–367.

Office of the Australian Information Commissioner. (2001, November). *Guidelines on privacy in the private health sector.* Retrieved from http://www.privacy.gov.au

Plessis, P.D., & Hirst, F.F. (2006). Written communication and counselling. In R. Bor & M. Watts (Eds.), *The trainee handbook: A guide for counselling and psychotherapy trainees* (2nd ed., pp. 91–109). London, England: Sage.

Privacy Act 1988 (Cth). Retrieved from www.comlaw.gov.au

Thomas, J.T. (2010). *The ethics of supervision and consultation: Practical guidance for mental health professionals.* Washington, DC: American Psychological Association.

Watts, P. (2009). *Surviving the witness box: Expert opinion in court.* Canning Bridge, WA: Ogilvie Publishing.

Chapter Ten

Stevens, B. (2008). *Crossfire! How to survive giving expert evidence as a psychologist.* Bowen Hills, Qld: Australian Academic Press.

Sun Tzu. (1988). *The art of war.* Boston, MA: Shambhala.

Watts, P. (2004). *A reliable witness.* Canning Bridge, WA: Ogilvie Publishing.

Watts, P. (2009). *Surviving the witness box: Expert opinion in court.* Canning Bridge, WA: Ogilvie Publishing. Revised and expanded from the 2004 book.

Chapter Eleven

Australian Government Department of Health. (2015). Better access to psychiatrists, psychologists and general practitioners through the MBS (Better Access) initiative. Retrieved from http://www.health.gov.au/internet/main/publishing.nsf/Content/mental-ba

Stevens, B.A. (2016). *Emotional learning: The way we are wired for intimacy.* Fremantle, WA: Fontaine Press.

Stevens, B.A. (2000). *Mirror, mirror: When self-love undermines your relationship.* Canberra, ACT: Canberra Clinical and Forensic Psychology.

Watts, P. (2014). *Internet pornography: Do-it-yourself treatment guide for men.* South Perth, WA: Ogilvie Publishing.

Chapter Twelve

American Counseling Association. (2005). *Buying and selling a private counseling practice.* Available from http://www.counseling.org/docs/private-practice-pointers/selling_or_buying_a_private_practice.pdf?sfvrsn=2

Australian Psychological Society. (n.d.). A practice contingency plan. In *The role of the APS in assisting an executor following the death of a psychologist.* Melbourne, Australia: Author.

Australian Psychological Society. (2014). *Selling or closing your practice: A guide for psychologists.* Melbourne, Australia: Author.

Barnett, J. E., Zimmerman, J., & Walfish, S. (2014). *The ethics of private practice: A practical guide for mental health clinicians.* New York, NY: Oxford University Press.

www.ingramcontent.com/pod-product-compliance
Lightning Source LLC
Chambersburg PA
CBHW050715280326

41926CB00088B/3042